# BEYOND
# STORY TIME...

201+ creative library program & fundraising plans
designed to invite EVERYONE into the library

by
Kathryn Kirkpatrick

*Kirkpatrick Publishing*

I dedicate this work to my fantastic family and to the shining stars in my life – my beautiful children, Nick and Aleah. With your support and encouragement, I've moved my writing from "dreamer" to "doer."
Thank you all so much!

# Forward

Why did I write this book? To help. I love libraries – always have. But, libraries need help. A long standing rock of nearly every community, rich in history and tradition, libraries are beginning to become polarizing entities, which is dangerous territory. Some are showplaces; visions of architectural genius and artistic masterpieces loved by the masses. Too many others are being defunded by those who can't see the library's value and are being overcome by apathy and maintenance issues.

The people are polarizing too. Dedicated bibliophiles work to uplift the community by supporting the library, while others have turned away, no longer reading for pleasure, or using their disposable income to purchase books or eBooks instead of embracing the glorious pleasure of not paying a cent for their literary materials. Some "experts" predict print books will not even be produced 10 years from now. I don't believe that, but even if it is true, with the right focus, there will always be a place for libraries.

Programming is a way to draw people into the library. I served for three years as the president of my Friends of the Library group and we had a great time coming up with new ways to get the community into the library. Information on programming ideas was difficult to find and any books I found were always slanted toward young children or teens and not toward everyone, making their value to a Friends group incomplete. The library belongs to EVERYONE and programming considerations should too. So I wrote this book as a comprehensive resource to use as a development tool to put together a programming plan that will reach all segments of the community. Some of the ideas presented may not be new to you, but I guarantee that some of them are new and that is what makes a comprehensive resource like this one so great. Library Friends have been creating great programming for their library patrons for years. I will share as many ideas as I have with you, and hope that they'll spark even more ideas for you and your community. There are many more than 201 ideas in here. As you read through, you'll see many programs that can be part of a series or further developed to stand alone on their own. For example, Program #98 has approximately 30 additional items cited that can be turned into programs. Use your creativity and knowledge of your own community demographic to build unique programs from the ideas presented.

So that's what this book is all about. It is about ways to breathe new life and interest within the community to come to the library. Come in for a program and hopefully leave with a renewed enthusiasm for "my library." The more relevant the library remains, the less likely it will be to fall prey to the budgetary axe.

Plans are written with libraries in mind, but can be adapted or modified for schools, churches, service organizations, community parks & recs, in some cases festivals, senior centers or any other group looking to get people together for a little fun, entertainment or education.

All of this great programming doesn't just happen. In many cases money is needed to either buy supplies or pay performers. Chapter 7 is dedicated to program ideas that will help generate revenue for library needs or other programs.

For the 201+ ideas, some are very straightforward and require no material or prep time. They are what librarians consider "passive programs." Other ideas require more prep and advertisement time, but will be worth the effort. Combine types so as not to over-tax the volunteers.

The greatest resource is our community. There are so many people with great talents or information that they could share, but no one ever asks them. Very often, people are more than willing to put together a short presentation and be open to questions which would help open up networking connections. One thing to be careful about though, presenters cannot openly promote their own business(es). They can say who they are and where they work, but can't sell their wares in the library or discuss the merits of their business vs. those of a competitor; there are rules about that kind of thing. Make sure to check with the library board before inviting business owners into the library.

In the immortal words of the great Mother Teresa, "Not all of us can do great things. But we can do small things with great love." So work hard dedicated Friends! Don't take for granted that the library will always be there. Use this book and make sure that the library remains a valuable asset of the community long into the future.

*"Without libraries what have we? We have no past and no future." - Ray Bradbury*

# Chapter 1 – Friends Groups & Programming Basics

## Friends Board

Every group needs to know why they exist. For Friends groups, we'll focus on the Vision and Mission Statements. Ever heard the phrase "Where do you see yourself in 5 years?" The answer is a vision statement.

Where the Vision Statement is the WHAT, the Mission Statement is the HOW. How will you achieve your vision? As an example, here are my vision and mission statements for the work you now hold in your hands. Vision – To see library Friends groups across the country work to foster a sense of need for their libraries within their own communities. Mission – Create and publish a comprehensive collection of great program ideas that Friends groups can use to achieve the vision. For a Friends group, let's look at some possibilities. (For Teen Council samples, see Chapter 3)

- Vision – Build a series of library programs that is a model for other similarly sized libraries to follow. Mission – Thoroughly develop and document "best practices" through refinement of library program series.
- Vision – Be considered the "hub" of the community. Mission – Provide as many gathering opportunities for all segments of the community as possible.
- Vision – Support the library in updating infrastructure and modernizing to support the growing population of the community. Mission – Pay for "X, Y & Z" by hosting 'fun'draising programs.

**Bylaws:** The bylaws include the vision and mission statements, but should be stated a bit more generally, so as to need revision less frequently. Also included in the bylaws:

- Membership
- Officer definition with duties
- Frequency of meetings and what happens at an annual meeting. It is important to stick to the stated schedule. An active Friends group should meet no less frequently than quarterly, with monthly being optimum to execute a year-round programming plan.
- Procedures (what constitutes a quorum etc.)

**Tax Status:** Check the rules. The majority of Friends groups are classified as 501(c)(3) groups and should file all required forms annually. Make this a priority.

**Friends:** The most important thing the Friends need? Ok, I really can't boil it down to one thing, so I'll focus on a few key needs:

- FOCUS – Start with Vision & Mission Statements to provide the needed framework for planning purposes.
- FORESIGHT – Be astute and aware of the "vibe" of the community. Keeping up isn't enough – stay ahead and give the community what they want <u>before</u> they even know they want it.
- ACTIVENESS – The Friends need to actively seek out and solicit information from patrons and community leaders on how they can more effectively serve the community. Ask.
- RESPONSIVENESS – Listening to and responding to feedback will make or break the credibility of a group. Providing a sense of ownership to patrons by responding to their suggestions (even if they aren't utilized) will create a positive relationship that is crucial.

**Volunteers:** A note about volunteers and where to find them. The short answer is everywhere! There are a lot of people who want to help, but are never asked, or they don't know what you need. Also, look to the high school. Many schools now require students to complete community service projects. Get the list of intended programs for the year to the school and recruit student volunteers as presenters or support staff for programs.

# Programming

Many programs will come to you as fee-for-service programs. It is important to evaluate the fee to its benefit. Is the program expensive, but will only serve a small audience? Then, it may not be the right fit. On the other hand, an expensive program that serves a small number of people may be perfectly acceptable if it grabs an underserved and targeted audience. Possibly the program is really expensive but can serve many and you don't have the space? Consider a larger venue like the elementary school with a flyer to parents so they know that the library sponsored the event. Perhaps it is cheap, but you don't think anyone will come? Either scrap the idea, or add food – food almost always gets 'em in! Don't forget to occasionally survey the patrons to ask what kind of programs they'd like to see in the library.

**Choosing Dates:** It is vital to have a good "finger on the pulse" of what's going on in the community and world. Planning a teen event on Prom weekend will most likely fail to generate the volume of teens who would normally attend. Scheduling a program that conflicts with another community event may not only reduce attendance, but could cause undue hurt feelings.

Consider the following when scheduling programs:
- School calendar
- School extra-curricular event calendars
- Community events
- Community arts and leisure calendars
- Local festivals
- State-wide and nation-wide holidays and events (think about opening day of fishing season, or how the Super Bowl may affect planned programs)

Community events that are designed to bring people into town all over, like a city-wide yard sale, or local business sidewalk sale, or sporting event, can easily be leveraged to generate traffic into the library. Consider how the Friends can enhance the enjoyment of visitors and possibly make a little money. See Chapter 7 for some ideas.

**Suggested timeline for programs:**
Most programs will work with the following timeline. Larger programs requiring more planning may need to have the timeline extended.

- 6 weeks prior – begin advertising. Do a "save the date" blog post and design print advertising.
- 4 weeks prior – Email the flyer to subscriber list for the age or interest group.
- 2 to 3 weeks prior – Send flyer and information to the newspaper and radio stations who have community events calendars. Make ¼ sheet flyers or bookmark flyers for the library staff to give out at the circulation desk.
- 1 week to a few days prior – Post a "reminder" blog post & create a prominent display in the library.

**Advertising:** The most vital piece of any library program is good advertising. Larger systems have advertising departments and require the Friends to use them to ensure quality and consistency. They charge the Friends a nominal fee for service. When using the advertising department, it is important to note that you'll be in competition with all the other branches for the advertising department's time, so get requests in early! If you don't have the luxury/restriction of an advertising department, you can design your own flyers for programs. Either way, you'll need to ensure that advertising includes all of the basic information of programs going on in the library.

- Date: Use full date, October 13, 2013 or Every Tuesday (if it is a series, put all the dates and what is planned each time). Example for College Readiness series:
  - November 1, 2013 – SAT Preparation
  - November 8, 2013 – Grants and Scholarships
  - November 15, 2013 – Selecting a major (career interest project)

- November 22, 2013 – Managing money (it doesn't all go to pizza!)
    - All programs run 6:00 – 7:00 pm
    - Snacks provided!
- Time: Use 1:00 – 3:00 (easier to read than 1 o'clock)
- Location: Be specific (Library meeting room, Teen Center, children's area)
- Eye catching graphics
- A quick synopsis of the program in one to two sentences & encouragement to attend

## Optional forms of advertising:

- Print: Flyers, bookmarks (very effective for series), posters (save posters for big events, or series – they are more expensive to produce and take up a lot of space), banners (use sparingly)
- Social Media: When it comes to the use of social media, there is a point where you can be _too_ present. If items are posted non-stop, you'll either be blocked or scrolled past. Manage saturation of social media and it can be a valuable tool. Save money by eliminating the need for some print advertising.
  Example: Post impromptu events, or events targeted to a small niche group (send a calendar invite to them and they'll feel special).
- Newspaper, Radio, TV, Chamber of Commerce: Utilize these resources for big events and fundraising activities. Does the library celebrate a birthday every year? These avenues will reach new potential patrons in a way that print advertising and social media alone, won't.
- Flash/Freeze mob: Works well to rally support for Teen programs. Consider this. We've all driven past teens with posters jumping up and down on the side of the road trying to coax us in for their fundraiser car wash, right? What would be the impact if those same teens, only more of them, had a big poster or banner and were standing still in some sort of odd, eye-catching formation? Think about it as a possibility.

- Outreach: Some systems still have bookmobiles, but many, many others have chosen to drop them for budget purposes. So what are other ways to take the library to the people? Visit schools, offer delivery service to home-bound folks, emergency responders, Veterans hospital or recovery center. Go green and do delivery via bicycle and you'll get great press! See program #181 for more information.

# Supply

**Initial Friends of the Library closet** (because you usually have little more than a closet) "stock"

- Pencils
- Permanent and erasable markers
- Crayons
- Temporary Tattoos (keep a nice variety for holidays etc.)
- Coloring sheets
- A variety of games (board and card)
- Scissors/Stapler/Staples/Tape/Tacks
- A cache of school sized scissors for children's programs
- Stationery with your logo for writing thank you notes
- Stamps
- A folding white board or easel
- Storage space for the Book Sale (Program #195)

**Some items of value for programs:**
The Friends may need some items that the library isn't funded for, or simply doesn't have. So, think about the programming plan for the year and work to acquire needed equipment through fundraising or donations. Possible purchases or needs include, but are not limited to:

- Audiovisual equipment
- Overhead mirror
- Pop-up tents/awnings
- Folding tables

- Additional chairs
- Reader boards
- Bulletin boards
- White board
- Smart board
- Easel

# Stumbling blocks to success:

- **Too many ideas, not enough money.** Fundraising really does need to be an integral piece of the annual plan. See Chapter 7 for some fundraising ideas. Whether fundraising is "small ball" or "gala style," there are gobs of ways to generate income. But let's say you live in a depressed area with little disposable income. What then? Look for programs with little to no cost. Believe me, there are plenty of them. Conduct a "time and talents" survey and see what community resources are available with no money. Hold a Supplies Drive to get art supplies, paper, audiovisual equipment, and other useful items. Hint: Do a supplies drive right at the end of school, when students are bringing home their left-overs from the school year. Money should never be a stumbling block that can't be overcome.

- **Too much interest, not enough space.** What a fantastic problem to have! Now is the time for partnerships, or on-going programs. For example, the Family game night (Program #165) is so successful that folks can't find space to play. Well, instead of once a month, make it the second and fourth Tuesdays instead and see how that goes. Or, the Puppet show (Program #27) was such a big hit last year, folks are still talking about it. Consider moving it to one of the elementary schools or community center where more people will be able to attend. You might think that moving a program defeats the purpose of getting people into the library, but with great follow-up it will actually enhance the credibility and approachability of the library, making the impression one of cooperation and inclusion. What if that Puppet show was scheduled close to the end of the school year and all of the people who came to the show also received their summer reading materials and a free magnet with the library's hours, as well as a list of planned summer programs? Cheaper than mailing all that stuff and would reach a whole lot of people in one shot.

- **The "Old Guard."** Ah, the "Yes, but..."gang. Love them, but not their vision. Their dedication to the group is admirable; however, their resistance to new ideas creates unnecessary drag. So how does a group handle someone like this? My recommendation in cases like this is to leverage the power of the survey. Let the voice of the people speak to support and overturn any "yeah, we tried that a few years ago and it didn't work," or "that is a good idea, but I don't think people will like that." Keep smiling and keep trying. Don't ever let one person, or a small faction of negativity bring down the group.

- **Great programs, no participants.** The first thing to do in a situation like this is to figure out what went wrong. Was it scheduling? Was it advertising? Was it not well planned? Or, did the program just "miss the mark?" Just because something has been tried and wasn't successful, doesn't mean that it is off the table forever. The idea had merit once. If you think it still does, modify and try again.

- **Over or under purchased supplies.** If storage space is available, over purchasing supplies is less of a problem. However, if the program was so specialized that the leftovers will sit and sit and may not ever be used, think about developing a program specifically around them, donating the supplies, or trading them for something else needed. Under purchasing is much more of a problem. Under purchasing supplies shows that the planning was less than perfect and leads to disappointment among the participants who came to the program, but couldn't participate due to lack of supplies. When a program relies on supplies, either make sure that there will be plenty, or require participants to register so that accurate numbers are available, then purchase at least 10 percent over to account for "can my friend come too?" or "oops. I made a mistake with this one, may I have another?" If the program is drop-in, make sure that advertising states something like "supplies are limited – first come, first served" or "while supplies last" which will let potential participants know that they may not get whatever is being offered, which softens the blow of disappointment.

All programs need to be recorded to be included in the Annual newsletter (Program #177). Cover the who, what, when, where and how, but also note ideas for next time.

The bottom line for any program at any time is expressing the value of the library for everyone. Let's look at some possibilities that may work for you at your library....

*"My two favourite things in life are libraries and bicycles. They both move people forward without wasting anything. The perfect day: riding a bike to the library."* - Peter Golkin

# Chapter 2 - Young Children and Families

Let's tackle the toughest crowd first. If you don't find a way to capture the attention of toddlers, preschoolers and elementary students, you'll never get their parents, grand-parents, baby-sitters, big brothers and big sisters. But, getting kids excited about coming to the library is going to take more than a weekly story time.

Technology has taken over and expands at an exponential rate. The young mind is wired differently than it was just a few generations ago. Young people require a higher and faster volume of stimulation than ever before. But, children are still natural bibliophiles. Start them young, capture their attention and they will be regular patrons for many, many years. With the right exposure, books will have as great a place in their lives as technologic "gizmos." Work to speak their language and embrace their exuberance. What I mean by that is, teach them to be respectful of the library's resources, but lay off the "shhh." Add in fabulous, engaging programming and you'll see them all the time.

A few programs that may entice young children and families to come to the library:

*"As a child, my number one best friend was the librarian in my grade school. I actually believed all those books belonged to her." Erma Bombeck*

# #1 – Get out there! A "free fun" exploration series

Family time is fun time! However, with the high saturation of electronics into the lives of young people, some of them seem to have forgotten how to have fun without a screen. This program series aims to not only explore screen free options, but even better, provide ideas for free, or nearly free activities. Rely on and challenge participants to brainstorm even more ideas.

**Target Audience:** Young children and families

**Things needed:**
- A Facilitator - someone to lead the discussion who is excited about the topic and has some ideas of their own
- Information about the activities discussed
- Audiovisual support (if needed)
- Activities for those children not interested in participating in the discussion/presentation (coloring sheets are a good option)

**Prep Time:** Minimal to arrange space and set out activity

**Program Time:** About an hour

**Number of Participants:** Limited only by space and fire code

**Number of Friends/Volunteers needed:** Facilitator and one volunteer to monitor the activity for those not participating in the discussion/presentation

**How/Notes:** How about discussing some of the following:
- Bug hunt
- Track down tracks. Looking for animal tracks in nature. Also consider talking about how to take an impression of a

track with Plaster of Paris, photograph them, or cut it out of mud.

- Be a tourist in your own home town. Many local attractions will offer discounts to residents, and an even deeper discount for providing a review. Sometimes attractions will even offer a resident "free day" as a thank you for their support.
- Letterboxing (Program #118)
- Camping
- Beachcombing
- The alphabet in nature - finding and taking photos of letters in nature – like this one. This type of photographic art has become quite popular and is fun to do with kids.

- Leaf collecting - do rubbings too and turn them into art projects to commemorate the family time.
- Family or neighborhood picnic
- Frisbee golf
- Visit places like a farm or fire station. With some advanced coordination these places are usually open for free tours.

# #2 – Hands-on chemistry series

When I think of chemistry, I think of lab coats, smoldering beakers, goggles and explosions. I know I'm not the only one. This program aims to introduce chemistry in a fun way to kids.

**Target Audience:** Children ages 5+

**Things needed:**
- An Instructor/Facilitator
- Audiovisual support (if needed)
- Needed supplies for the day's experiment
- An instruction sheet to follow and take home so participants can teach family and friends, which furthers the level of their understanding of the concept.

**Prep Time:** Will depend on the activity chosen

**Program Time:** An hour – make sure that the activity includes a discussion about "what's happening," but make sure there is time for the activity. The 'what's happening' discussion may need to happen while the participants are engaged in the activity.

**Number of Participants:** Limited only by space and supplies, but registration is recommended.

**Number of Friends/Volunteers needed:** 1-2

**How/Notes:** Make sure to let participants know that everything they see and touch has the ability to change. Sometimes substances change to form new substances. This is called a chemical change. Other times substances change but keep the same identity. This is called a physical change. Do some experiments with both types of changes.

Ideas:
- Make toothpaste

- Make a lava lamp
- Make ice cream in a bag
- Make slime
- Disappearing ink

Think about offering this as a weekly summer series with cold drinks afterwards.

*"The world is full of magical places, and the library has always been one of them for me. A library can be that special place for our children." - Julie Andrews*

# #3 – The natural world series

The wonders of the world around us are amazing. And to the target audience for this series, they are also undiscovered. Have fun introducing the natural world with this adaptable "recipe" of a story, song & craft.

**Target Audience:** Ages 1-pre-K

**Things needed:**
- A Facilitator/Storyteller
- A story
- A song
- A craft – plus supplies to support chosen craft
- The library's resources on the topic
- Fun facts (2-3 on a take-home sheet to further peak interest)

**Prep Time:** ½ hour or so to pull and arrange the library's resources, arrange space and set up craft.

**Program Time:** An hour

**Number of Participants:** Limited by space and craft resources purchased. Recommend registration.

**Number of Friends/Volunteers needed:** 2, including Facilitator

**How/Notes:** Run the series either once a week for a few months, every other week for a quarter & repeat, or once a month for a year. Frequency will depend on other programs at the library or other community offerings for this age group.
Program ideas for the series:
- Buggy for bugs
  - Book: _The very hungry caterpillar_ by Eric Carle, _Hey, Little Ant_ by Phillip M. Hoose
  - Song: Itsy, bitsy spider

- o   Craft: craft pipe cleaners into spiders
- The Night Sky
  - o   Book: *Zoo in the Sky: A Book of Animal Constellations* by Jacqueline Mitton
  - o   Song: Twinkle, twinkle, little star
  - o   Craft: Stamp art using space stamps
- Fly birdie, fly! (bird migration)
  - o   Book: *In the Nest* by Anna Milbourne or *Baby Bird* by Joyce Dunbar
  - o   Song: Hey Mrs. Bird or teach the Chicken Dance
  - o   Craft: Homemade bird feeder.
  - o   Need:
    - ▪   Sugar ice cream cone
    - ▪   Pipe cleaner
    - ▪   Table knife
    - ▪   Creamy peanut butter
    - ▪   Circle oat cereal (like Cheerios®)
    - ▪   Birdseed
    - ▪   Poke a hole in the end of the ice cream cone. Twist a knot in the end of the pipe cleaner. Thread the pipe cleaner into the ice cream cone and out the hole (the knot will hold the pipe cleaner in place). Use the table knife to spread peanut butter on the outside of the cone. Press or roll the cereal and birdseed into the peanut butter. Hang in yard for winter guests.
- Sea Creatures
  - o   Book: *The Rainbow Fish* by Marcus Pfister, *Baby Beluga* by Ashley Wolf Raffi, *In the Ocean* by AJ Wood
  - o   Song: Down by the Bay or Somewhere in the Ocean
  - o   Craft: Sea salt art (2 teaspoons of salt to one teaspoon liquid starch + food coloring) Make several colors and let participants paint an outlined fish, octopus, shark etc.)

- Weather
  - Book: _Froggy Gets Dressed_ by Jonathan London, _The Wind Blew_ by Pat Hutchins, _Rain_ by Mary Stojic
  - Song: Rain, rain, go away or Mr. Sun
  - Craft: Use markers to draw colored arcs onto ½ a coffee filter, then paint over them with water. Or make wind socks. Make a top out of a piece of decorated construction paper, then glue streamers of crepe paper to the bottom. Attach a string at the top for hanging.
- Changing Seasons
  - Book: _Four Seasons Make a Year_ by Anne Rockwell
  - Song: 4 Seasons in a Year
  - Craft: Draw and label a quad picture of a tree in each season
- Animals of the North
  - Book: _A Caribou Alphabet_ by Mary Beth Owens
  - Song: The North Wind
  - Craft: Moose puppets (paper bags, and hand tracing antlers)
- Living Desert
  - Book: _Deep in the Desert_ by Rhonda Lucas Donald, _Creatures of the Desert World_ A National Geographic action book
  - Song: Animals in the Desert (to the tune of Wheels on the Bus)
  - Craft: Sand molds, or making snakes from beads and pipe cleaners or paper chains
- Rocks & Fossils
  - Book: _Fossils tell of long ago_ by Aliki, _The Rock Factory: a story about the rock cycle_ by Jacqui Bailey and Matthew Lilly
  - Song: Do you know the rocks I know? (to the tune of the Muffin Man)
  - Craft: "Fossil" imprints. Use play dough and leaves to make imprints in the play dough, put a hole in

the top. Allow to dry and provide a pretty ribbon or yarn for hanging at home.

- Rain Forest
  - o Book: _The Umbrella_ by Jan Brett, _Verdi_ by Janelle Cannon, _The Mixed up Chameleon_ by Eric Carle
  - o Song: The little green frog
  - o Craft: Wooden snakes are available in bulk and are fun to paint, or make a snake or frog from clay, or decorate a parrot outlined on a piece of paper.
- Trees & their creatures
  - o Book: _A tree is nice_ by Janice May Udry, _Who lives in a tree?_ By Susan Canizares
  - o Song: The leaves on the tree
  - o Craft: Do tree rubbing. Children work in pairs and take bark rubbings from trees outside. Or, lay a leaf on a piece of paper and let the participants use a toothpick to poke an outline and the veins onto their paper.
- In bloom – seasonal plants
  - o Book: _Planting a Rainbow_ by Lois Ehlert, _Jack's Garden_ by Henry Cole, _How a seed grows_ by Helen J. Jordan
  - o Song: Flowers Growing (sung to the tune of Mulberry Bush)
  - o Craft: Plant a seed in a cup to take home (bean in a cup), or decorate a small flower pot and plant a seed.

# #4 – How things work series

Ever wonder how popcorn pops, or why a Frisbee flies (or in my case flies poorly)? This series is dedicated to answering, scientifically, how things work. Make sure to keep things age appropriate, at say, the 3$^{rd}$ grade level and add a fun activity to accompany the lesson, so that participants don't realize they are actually learning something.

**Target Audience:** School aged children and families

**Things needed:**
- An Instructor/Facilitator – Recommend partnering with a local Science teacher to secure top-notch Science students looking to pad their college applications with community service.
- Needed supplies – will vary depending on the topic discussed
- Audiovisual support – recommended, as a simple slide show presentation will help solidify the concepts and will reach the visual learners

**Prep Time:** Will vary depending on the topic

**Program Time:** An hour

**Number of Participants:** Recommend registration on this, so that supplies are not over or under purchased.

**Number of Friends/Volunteers needed:** 1-2, including Instructor/Facilitator

**How/Notes:** Recommend this program run on a weekly, or bi-weekly basis.
A few ideas to get started:
- Compass – Use it to follow a land navigation course outside, or inside if the weather is bad. Ask questions like

"What is on the wall at 174 degrees?" "If you walk 45 steps on a 105 degree azimuth, what do you run into?"

- Kaleidoscope – make and take one home (will need to purchase supplies)
- Popcorn poppers – use and eat!
- Pens (ball point vs. gel vs. marker) – take one with the Friends logo
- Locks & handcuffs – Have the local police discuss these and allow participants to practice with them
- 3-D movie – Watch a short one
- Frisbee – play with it outside
- Spinning top – play and take (will need to purchase quality tops)
- Kite – make and take (will need to purchase supplies)
- Mirrors – decorate and take framed mirrors (will need to purchase supplies)
- Parachute – play some games (use the one(s) from the parachute play program (Program #22))
- Solar & wind energy – make a list together of possible applications in everyday life.
- Noisemakers – Just take!
- Cartoons – Watch one or two. Maybe a cool old one and a modern day one and contrast them.
- Pencil sharpener – Use it to sharpen all of the Library staff's pencils, then take one home with the Friends logo on it
- Automatic door – do this one only if the library has an automatic door, otherwise, the hands-on effect will be lost
- Bicycle – ask participants to bring one and go for a quick ride
- Yo-yo – practice and take (will need to purchase)
- Stringed instruments – practice playing some (borrow from Music department or have local music shop owner demo)

The list could go on and on, of course; these are just a few ideas that would work in the library and conceptually aren't too difficult for the target age group.

# #5 - Read to animals

An article in Everyday Health by Silvia Foti writing for Web Vet, notes that reading to animals is both calming and confidence building when applied to reluctant and/or emergent readers. Getting reluctant or emergent readers into the library and pairing them with a dog or cat will help them tremendously. Getting a program like this off the ground may be a bit tricky, but once established, will likely be well received and there will be a waiting list of future participants.

**Target Audience:** 6-12 year old reluctant and emergent readers

**Things needed:**
- A gentle dog or cat with handler
- A willing reader
- A quiet space with comfy chairs or bean bags
- Great reading material
- Treats for both reader and animal

**Prep Time:** Once set up, this program becomes routine. The initial preparation comes in finding animals suitable for the task and finding readers who could benefit from the program. Print flyers aren't necessary, but a blog post or email to the local elementary and middle schools might help generate interest. For the program itself, the library staff should prepare some recommended reading materials, or participants can bring their own.

**Program Time:** Plan on 30 minutes per reader per session. A 1½ - 2 hour run time for the animal and handler, 30 minutes per child with 3-4 readers participating. Recommend this program be scheduled for early Saturday morning before the library is too full, or maybe even before it opens.

**Number of Participants:** Up to 3-4 per week, per animal participating. Registration is required for this program.

**Number of Friends/Volunteers needed:** 1 + animal and handler

**How/Notes:**
Get recommendations for participants and invite them.

Register participants for a time slot. Recommend the program run for 4 weeks each session, which will enable more readers to participate and 4 weeks is enough time to generate some enthusiasm for establishment of a lifetime love of reading.

- Meet and greet animal
- Settle in and read

** Accidents do happen. Work hard to get animals suitable for this role, but consideration should be given to a liability waiver that the participant's parents/guardians sign allowing them to participate in the program and releasing the library from responsibility if there is an issue.

# #6 – Music programs

Local musicians are the best because they are usually not too expensive, or even sometimes free if they are looking to try out new material. Also, look for ethnic musicians that use music to tell stories (double-whammy – especially if the instruments are unique and the participants are allowed to touch them) Consider coupling an ethnic music presentation with a cultural food experience (Program #99).

**Target Audience:** Young children

**Things needed:**
- A musician with fun music
- Books to accompany the music style presented (optional – a simple library display will also aid in promotion of the program)
- Floor space for dancing
- Snacks (optional)

**Prep Time:** Minimal to arrange space

**Program Time:** 45 minutes to an hour

**Number of Participants:** Limited only be space and fire code

**Number of Friends/Volunteers needed:** 1

**How/Notes:** Make sure that any music presented is an interactive experience with participants asked to sing along or shout out.

If the music is on a theme, ensure that all of the library's materials are available on the subject so that participants make the book/music/topic connection.

# #7 – Travel topics – Disney with kids

If you are going to spend your hard-earned money on a vacation like Disney Land/World, you'd probably like to make the most of it. "Should I stay at a Disney property?" "Should I buy a Park Hopper Pass?" "When is the best time to go?" "How long should we stay?" Tons of questions and you know you need a plan. There is surely a Disney "guru" in town who would be glad to put together a presentation of tips and tricks, offer advice and field questions about their experiences with the Magic Kingdom.

**Target Audience:** Young children and families

**Things needed:**
- A Presenter or Facilitator. Solicit a volunteer through social media.
- Audiovisual support (if needed)
- Coloring sheets (Disney perhaps?) to keep young ones entertained during the presentation/discussion. Or show a Disney movie in another area.
- A list of websites and resources

**Prep Time:** Less than ½ hour to arrange space

**Program Time:** Plan on an hour, but make sure to have the space available if the program runs long.

**Number of Participants:** Limited only by space and fire code. The speaker may have a preference, in which case registration would be recommended.

**Number of Friends/Volunteers needed:** 1 to keep the coloring sheets moving or maybe read a Disney story

**How/Notes:** This presentation is best covered as a tips & tricks / dos & don'ts style presentation with about ½ the time dedicated to discussion and questions.

The volume of information on this topic can be daunting. So much so it could make your head spin. But, if you were to go to Disney Land/World without a plan, you'd probably wish you had done a little homework first. People coming to this program will likely have horror stories to tell, so be ready for that. For every tip & trick, there are just as many "Don't let this happen to you!" stories, which are valuable too.

*"Libraries are the local portal to anywhere, everywhere, past, present and future." - Karin Kallmaker*

# #8 – Rhythmic clapping and chanting

Young children are total body learners. They love to move and this program is tailor-made for them. Bring in a few drums, find some fun songs and begin to teach the foundations of language through rhythm and repetition. This program will help develop important language and coordination skills by giving participants practice with active listening, cooperation, following directions, hand-eye coordination and respect for themselves and others. All good stuff, and fun too!

**Target Audience:** 0-4 year olds (the very young will still benefit from the music and smiling faces)

**Things needed:**
- A Facilitator/Teacher
- Music & music player
- Drums or other fun rhythm makers
- A lesson plan
- Snacks (optional)

**Prep Time:** Minimal to arrange space and set up music

**Program Time:** This crowd will respond well for about 30 minutes.

**Number of Participants:** Limited only by space and fire code. Be aware that participants will need space to move.

**Number of Friends/Volunteers needed:** 1 if serving snacks, otherwise the Facilitator/Teacher can handle this program.

**How/Notes:** This could be done weekly for a month with a new sound each time, or the same program could be repeated once a quarter or twice a year to capture a new audience. The demographic of the area will dictate the need. Try songs like:

- A sailor went to sea, sea, sea to see what he could see, see, see. But all that he could see, see, see was the bottom of the deep blue sea, sea, sea
- Miss Mary Mac
- If you're happy and you know it

Also try presenting several different rhythm makers like Lummi sticks, maracas, drums and castanets.

Check out _Rhythm Play_ by Kenya Masala for more ideas.

As a follow-on activity, how about giving participants open markers and paper and have them draw to the beat.

# #9 – PJs at the library

Kids love going out in their jammies! What could be more fun than bringing a blanket and favorite "stuffie" and coming to the library for a few bedtime stories? This simple program will have kids begging to wear their jammies to the library – even in the middle of the day.

**Target Audience:** Young children and families

**Things needed:**
- Reader
- Soothing music & music player
- Low lights
- Bedtime stories

**Prep Time:** Just enough to turn the lights down a bit, turn on some music and grab a few wonderful books.

**Program Time:** Approximately 30 minutes

**Number of Participants:** Limited only by space and fire code

**Number of Friends/Volunteers needed:** 1

**How/Notes:** Let participants get comfortable & read great stories. Recommend setting out a selection of other bed-time stories and leaving the circulation desk open for a few minutes at the end of the program. This will increase circulation tremendously.

Additionally, recommend this program run every other week, which will increase the turn-over of materials, as participants will return the materials they checked out last time and take new items.

# #10 – Healthy eating collage placemat

Young children learn about their world through the things they hear, see and touch. This program gives them an opportunity to create their own visual reference about healthy eating. Discuss "green light, yellow light & red light" foods, and what healthy eating means.

**Target Audience:** 4-9 year olds

**Things needed:**
- An Instructor/Facilitator
- A large variety of magazines with food pictures
- Construction paper or card stock in red, yellow and green
- Glue
- Clear contact paper
- Stickers
- Markers
- Scissors (one per person)

**Prep Time:** Time to gather magazines. Plus about ½ hour to cut contact paper and lay out supplies.

**Program Time:** About an hour

**Number of Participants:** Recommend this be limited to fewer than 15, as they'll need room to spread out. Even if there is plenty of room, they'll make a big mess.

**Number of Friends/Volunteers needed:** 1 for fewer than 10 participants, 2 for more than 10 participants

**How/Notes:** To make the healthy eating placemat collage, prepare a background with three sections of red, yellow, green construction paper or card stock. Provide a supply of food pictures cut from magazines, plus additional magazines to go through.

Participants choose photos and decide which category they belong in, then paste onto their placemat. Cover placemats with clear contact paper.

Recommend asking for magazine donations or asking for out-of-circulation items.

*"Having fun isn't hard when you've got a library card."*
*[ARTHUR] – PBS Kids*

# #11 – Paint & race – wooden cars

This program pays homage to the Boy Scout's tradition of the Pinewood Derby. Here, the cars are provided and participants paint & adorn them, then race. A short physics discussion could be included in the program, but keep it basic & appropriate to the audience.

**Target Audience:** Young children & families

**Things needed:**
- Facilitators to help with painting and racing
- Small wooden unfinished cars (see How/Notes)
- A track – Check with the local Boy Scout Council to see if they have one available to borrow or use plastic car track (make sure it is elevated and the cars fit in it)
- Acrylic paint & brushes
- Stickers
- Small prizes for racers (race tattoos, die cast cars, ribbons)
- Tournament Board

**Prep Time:** Time to acquire track & supplies and test the track. Set up for program will be about an hour (½ hour to an hour to set up the track, and ½ hour to set out supplies and set up workspaces).

**Program Time:** Approximately 2 hours – will depend on the number of racers.

**Number of Participants:** Recommend registration to ensure an adequate amount of supplies.

**Number of Friends/Volunteers needed:** At least 2

**How/Notes:** A trial run of the cars is vital! It won't be fun if the cars don't fit in the track, or fall off halfway through the race. Slope should be from 30 degrees to zero degrees over a run of 12 feet.

There is a lot of information and resources available at
*http://www.abc-pinewood-derby.com*

Tournament brackets can be found at
*http://www.printyourbrackets.com*

Wooden cars can be found at *http://www.amazon.com* (the open wheel, Indy style in packs of 12) or
*http://www.orientaltrading.com* (old fashioned, open wheel style in packs of 12)

# #12 - Lego® building demonstration

I don't know anyone who doesn't like Legos®. Even parents, who have experienced the unique joy of stepping on a Lego® in the middle of the night, still harbor an affinity for those little colorful blocks of wonder. The imagination and creativity that comes from working with Legos® works its way into other creative outlets like mechanics, writing, drawing, cooking and monster fort building. Bring in someone or a group to demonstrate some creative possibilities with Legos® and this program will be _very_ well attended.

**Target Audience:** Young children - Tweens

**Things needed:**
- A Presenter/Facilitator
- Extra Legos®
- Example project sheets (optional)
- Workspace

**Prep Time:** Minimal to set up space

**Program Time:** An hour

**Number of Participants:** Will be limited by available space and extra Legos®. Recommend registration if space is tight.

**Number of Friends/Volunteers needed:** 1 + Presenter/Facilitator

**How/Notes:** Have the Presenter/Facilitator show various tips and tricks with the Legos®. It would also be beneficial to have a few finished pieces (not from kits) available for participants to look at and try to emulate.

Legos® are for children 3+, as the small pieces are choking hazards. Be aware of that when inviting the very young in for this program.

# #13 – Sing-song spelling time

My nieces, adorable identical twins, love to go to a program at their library called Pre-School Story time. Lots of libraries have a program like this, and I asked them what they loved most about theirs. They described learning spelling words reconfigured on the B-I-N-G-O song. Consider this: "There was a bear eating bamboo and PANDA was his name oh, P-A-N-D-A..." Think of the possibilities of building a program around singing and spelling.

**Target Audience:** 3-6 year olds

**Things needed:**
- A Facilitator
- Stories about the song that week
- The other books from the library collection to accompany the song topic

**Prep Time:** Minimal - only to pull library materials

**Program Time:** 30 minutes to an hour

**Number of Participants:** A good size for a group like this is about 15-20, but there really is no limit, just the fire code.

**Number of Friends/Volunteers needed:** 1

**How/Notes:** Try:
- In the glen, I see a sight and HORSE is her name oh...
- At the tracks, I hear a noise, it's coming from the TRAIN oh...
- These two things, go on my feet, and SHOES are their name oh...

Put out a suggestion box for clever and creative parents and caregivers to drop in their ideas too.

# #14 – All about pets

Responsible pet ownership begins with readiness. The percentage of pets in shelters due to "we just didn't realize..." is very high. Arm interested patrons with the knowledge they need to choose and care for a "best friend."

**Target Audience:** Children ages 5+ and families

**Things needed:**
- An Instructor/Facilitator - Consider inviting the local vet or pet store owner as a speaker, as well as other kids who have pets who can speak about what is involved in animal care
- Audiovisual support (if needed)
- A dog or cat (optional, of course but, if the discussion includes grooming, a live model would be nice)

**Prep Time:** Minimal to arrange space

**Program Time:** An hour

**Number of Participants:** Registration recommended if animals come. Otherwise, limited only by space and fire code

**Number of Friends/Volunteers needed:** 1

**How/Notes:** Make sure to include the following topics:
- What does it mean to "be ready"
- Choosing a breed
- Caring – Feeding, cleaning, leaving home alone
- Training – Obedience, tricks
- The importance of play
- Grooming

# #15 – Hand-sewing

Beginning sewing can be accomplished in many ways. This program will be developed depending on the age, interest and space available for young sewers. A sample project is presented here (See How/Notes), but the possibilities for projects in this program are plentiful.

**Target Audience:** 5-12 year olds

**Things needed:**
- An Instructor – ask for a volunteer and develop the project together.
- Craft felt or fabric
- Embroidery needles and embroidery floss in a variety of colors
- Scissors
- A template (make a simple bone or fish template)
- Fill (poly or natural fiber, rags etc.)

**Prep Time:** About an hour – ½ hour to arrange space and set out supplies and ½ hour to cut a few felt/fabric sets to use for demonstration

**Program Time:** 1 – 1 ½ hours

**Number of Participants:** Limited by Instructor preference (recommend registration if needed)

**Number of Friends/Volunteers needed:** At least 2, including the Instructor

**How/Notes:** Sample project:

This project will benefit the canine and feline friends in the neighborhood animal shelter and participants will work extra hard knowing that their work will be enthusiastically destroyed by a doggie or kitty in need.

The first step is to cut out the felt pieces (two matching are needed and need not be the same color)

Next, choose a floss color and thread the needle (make sure to knot the end).

Show a whipstitch and a blanket stitch, both appropriate for joining pieces together.

Instruct participants to leave an opening 2" wide so that the figure can be stuffed.

This project looks cute whether it is turned or not. Discuss what it means to turn the seams to the inside and decide, based on the participants, whether or not to turn.

Stuff with fill (If giving to animals, make sure to use only natural fill, as it is dangerous for animals to ingest poly-fill)

Close the gap with the same kind of stitch used to go around the rest of the project.

OPTIONAL: If sending the completed projects to the local animal shelter, discuss whether it is ok or not to put a dry treat or a piece of catnip inside before closing.

# #16 – Terrariums

This project is a fantastic family art project and would be a great addition to a series dedicated to families working together creatively. How about doing this project right before Mother's Day?

**Target Audience:** Families

**Things needed:**
- Miscellaneous glass containers
- Cups and funnels
- Charcoal
- Sand (Colored sand adds a nice touch)
- Rocks (pea gravel works)
- Soil
- Small plants
- Graphic depicting the order in which supplies are filled in with approximate amounts
- Tablecloths or newspaper to protect the work surface

**Prep Time:** An hour at the library, plus time to gather materials prior to the event

**Program Time:** This is an "at your own pace" program, but it really only takes about 15 minutes to finish, so think about varying the start times. Half the group starts at the top of the hour, the other half at the half hour mark. Make sure registration sheets note that it is not necessary to arrive exactly at the assigned time.

**Number of Participants:** Will depend on the size of the facility and amount of available supplies. Registration will be required. Have enough containers, so that there are plenty of extras in case of breakage. Separate available extras per time slot, so that each time slot has some overage. Then, if a family would like to do another, and there are still containers left, the answer can be "yes".

**Number of Friends/Volunteers needed:** 2-3. One at check-in, and one to help with the charcoal (it really is too messy to leave out), and one to assist with the sand (kids like to go overboard with this section, so it is nice to have a volunteer to remind them that they need to leave room for soil and plants.

**How/Notes:** This requires a variety of glass containers, soil, charcoal, colored sand, rocks and plants. Use cups and funnels for getting the "ingredients" in and a chart to explain that the charcoal goes in first. It is a great project to do right before Mother's Day which encourages male participation in preparation for Mom's big day.

Consider the size of the space and the number of supplies you are willing to purchase. It is possible to get the soil and some of the sand and beautiful rocks for free, and look in the local thrift stores to find all kinds of funky glass containers (they have to be open enough to fit the plant in - think fish bowl style)

Make sure to layer in the charcoal first. Then, rocks, sand, dirt and plants. When finished, the terrarium should look a little like this one:

# #17 – Countdown to Kindergarten

Kindergarten – So exciting! Hopefully the new kindergarteners who will come to this program are already regular library patrons. Whether they are or not, make sure that the countdown festivities include a tour of books that will be of interest to them as they begin to read.

**Target Audience:** Incoming kindergarteners and their families

**Things needed:**
- Activities. Needed supplies will depend on activities chosen (See How/Notes below)
- Upbeat music
- Stories
- Snacks (optional but recommended)

**Prep Time:** An hour to set up stations and arrange space

**Program Time:** 2 hours

**Number of Participants:** Limited only by space and fire code

**Number of Friends/Volunteers needed:** Several. The number will depend on number of activities chosen.

**How/Notes:** This program could take on a life of its own. When brainstorming activities and games to play, the possibilities are countless. Consider including some of the following:
- Teacher talk – ask a local Kindergarten teacher or retired Kindergarten teacher to discuss some of the things to expect in Kindergarten. Let the kids ask as many questions as they want.
- Games:
    o How fast can you? (Get dressed, pack your lunch, pack your school bag)
    o What time is it?

- Lace it up – have practice boards for learning how to lace up shoes
  - Match the snack – have healthy and not-so-great choices and have the children choose which one is which
  - How many words? Post the word "KINDER" on a long piece of butcher paper. Gather the children together and make a list of all of the words they can think of that start with the sounds in each of the letters. Don't worry about the K/C sound questions, just write the words correctly. Tell them that learning about the K & C sounds is one of the wonderful things they'll learn very soon!
- Crafts:
  - Make a "get ready" chart
  - Make a "Time to" clock. Combine these two and draw pictures of what their morning clock will look like at certain points in the "getting ready" process.
- Story – _Countdown to Kindergarten_ by Alison McGhee
- Hang numbers from 10 to 1 on sheets of copy paper in a row. People will think they are just decorations until the end of the party when they'll be used to count down, New Year's Eve style. Select 10 parents and the managing librarian to participate. Everyone shouts out the number and a parent pulls it off the wall until they get to "one", then the managing librarian yells "Happy Kindergarten!" and reveals a "Happy Kindergarten" banner. Or, leave out the banner and just have everyone shout "Happy Kindergarten!"

Check out _www.education.com_, for more ideas.

# #18 – Cookies in a jar

Sing it now, "Who stole the cookies from the cookie jar?" Answer – No one! This program will give participants a chance to put cookies IN the cookie jar by preparing a gift for someone special.

**Target Audience:** Young children and families

**Things needed:**
- Quart size glass canning jars with clean lids
- Measuring spoons & cups
- Bowls or plastic lined shallow boxes
- Cookie ingredients
- Fabric squares
- Ribbon or jute
- Labels
- Pre-printed recipe cards
- Hole punch
- Food handling gloves (optional but recommended)
- Stickers and markers

**Prep Time:** ½ hour to an hour to set up filling stations

**Program Time:** Since it doesn't take too long to put the jars together, recommend this be a drop-in program scheduled for a few hours or as part of a larger program. Maybe a story time or movie could be included?

**Number of Participants:** Recommend registration if it is a stand-alone program (assign times to registrants – example the first 20 are assigned 1000-1030, the next 20, 1030-1100 and so on). Number of participants will depend on materials purchased and space available. Or, if you'd like, don't put a limit on the number of registrants and purchase the materials after registration closes.

**Number of Friends/Volunteers needed:** 1 per type of cookie

**How/Notes:** Recommend one jar per child. Post an allergen notice at registration and away from the food so allergy sufferers can turn away before exposure.

Recommend 1-2 tables per type of cookie depending on the number of participants.

Entertain the idea of conducting this program prior to Mother's Day, Father's Day or Teacher Appreciation Week in May. Tie-in with Teacher Thank You Letters (Program #24) and there will be some awfully thankful teachers in the neighborhood.

This program could also be used as a holiday time fundraiser. Try:

**Cowboy Cookie Mix in a Jar:**
Layer the following in a quart size jar in the order given. Press layers firmly in place before adding the next ingredient.
1 ⅓ cup rolled oats
½ cup packed brown sugar
½ cup white sugar
½ cup chopped pecans (or any kind of nut)
1 cup semisweet chocolate chips
1 ⅓ cup all-purpose flour
1 teaspoon baking soda
¼ teaspoon salt

Include a card that says: COWBOY COOKIES – Preheat oven to 350 degrees F (175 degrees C). Grease cookie sheets. In a medium bowl, mix together ½ cup melted butter or margarine, 1 egg, and 1 teaspoon vanilla. Stir in the entire contents of the jar. Feel free to use hands to finish mixing, the mixture will be thick! Shape into walnut sized balls. Place 2 inches apart on prepared cookie sheets. Bake for 11 to 13 minutes in the preheated oven. Transfer from cookie sheets to cool on wire racks. Makes about 1 ½ dozen cookies.

**Sand Art Cookies:**

Layer the following in a quart size jar in the order given. Press layers lightly in place before adding the next ingredient.

½ cup white sugar

½ cup rolled oats

½ cup candy-coated chocolate pieces (like M&Ms®)

1 ¼ cups all-purpose flour

½ teaspoon baking powder

½ teaspoon salt

½ cup crispy rice cereal

½ cup semisweet chocolate chips

Include a card that says: Preheat oven to 350 degrees F (175 degrees C). Grease a cookie sheet. Empty the entire contents of the jar into a medium bowl. Add 1 large egg and ½ cup melted margarine; mix well. Form dough into 1 inch balls and bake for 10 to 12 minutes. Makes about 2 dozen cookies.

**Country Oatmeal Cookies:**

Layer the following in a quart size jar in the order given. Press layers firmly in place before adding the next ingredient.

¾ cup white sugar

¾ cup brown sugar

1 cup rolled oats

1 ½ cups all-purpose flour

1 ½ teaspoons baking powder

½ teaspoon salt

1 cup semisweet chocolate chips (or raisins)

1 cup chopped walnuts (or pecans)

Include a card that says: Preheat oven to 350 degrees F (175 degrees C). In a medium bowl, cream together ¾ cup of softened butter or margarine, 2 eggs and 1 teaspoon vanilla. Add the entire contents of the jar, and mix by hand until combined. Drop dough by spoonful onto an ungreased cookie sheet. Bake for 12 to 15 minutes. Transfer from cookie sheets to cool on wire racks. Makes about 1 ½ dozen cookies.

# #19 – A snowy day in summer

Who thinks about winter in the middle of summer? Mid-summer when the kids are cranky because they are bored, thoughts of winter might be kind of fun. Think of creating a Winter Wonderland in the library and enjoying some of the delights of snow and winter. How about a crumpled paper ball fight? A few crafts like: cotton ball snowmen, ornament making or home-made wrapping paper making? Decorate with paper snowflakes, line the floor with old sheets or inexpensive white tablecloths. Enjoy cocoa and decorating sugar cookies, then head back out into the summer heat.

**Target Audience:** Young children and families to everyone

**Things needed:**
- Cocoa
- Winter stories with dynamic storyteller
- Winter music
- Paper, scissors, pipe cleaners, string (for making and hanging snowflakes)
- Cotton balls, glue & construction paper & markers (for snowmen)
- Sugar cookies & decorative icings and sprinkles
- Movie – *Frosty the Snowman* or *Snow Buddies*?
- White tablecloths (optional)

**Prep Time:** About an hour to set up all the stations

**Program Time:** 2 -3 hours

**Number of Participants:** Limited only by space and supplies. Registration is recommended if space is tight, otherwise an Open House format works well.

**Number of Friends/Volunteers needed:** Several

**How/Notes:** This program works well as a station to station program with the movie as the culminating event, starting at the 1 ½ hour mark (or backwards from the program end time).

Suggested stations:
- Snowflake making (paper and pipe cleaners)
- Snowman making and decorating (construction paper and felt)
- Sugar cookie decorating
- Winter storytelling
- Snowman soup making (cocoa, mini-marshmallows, small wrapped chocolate drop candies, small wrapped candy canes) put all ingredients into a sandwich size zip-style bag with a label that says "Snowman Soup"
- "Snowball" fight (crumpled up paper)
- Homemade wrapping paper making

# #20 - A beach day in winter

For those who live on the coast of Florida, Texas, California or Hawaii, this program may not make the yearly program list. But, for dwellers in Nebraska, Minnesota, Wisconsin, Montana, Alaska, or any other place where long about the end of February, people have become so grouchy that they'd rather pull their hair out strand by strand than see one more flake of snow – this program is splendid! Turn the library into a beach oasis for the day. Leave the boots and snow pants at the door and have some fun in the sun!

**Target Audience:** Children and families

**Things needed:** This list is only limited by the imagination, space and budget. Decorate to the hilt, or just bring in a few extra lights & throw out some beach towels & beach balls – the choice is yours. A meeting room can be totally transformed, while a party in the stacks may need to be scaled back a bit. Here are a few starter thoughts:
- Music – tropical, of course
- Lights – heat lamps or LEDs. (if heat lamps are used, keep them out of reach of little hands)
- Punch
- Shells on the "beach" (sand colored paper)
- Plastic critters to play with on the "beach"
- Paper palm trees
- Beach towels and umbrellas (space permitting)
- Sugar cookies to decorate shaped like tropical fish, hibiscus flowers, or the sun

**Prep Time:** A few hours to several days depending on the "intensity level" of the party

**Program Time:** 2-3 hours

**Number of Participants:** Limited only by the fire code. As it is with any open program, set a "planning number" for purchase of supplies. If you go over and run out of everything, thank profusely, apologize and bring out the back-up stuff (coloring sheets related to the theme). Or, require registration to ensure adequate supplies. Either way is fine.

**Number of Friends/Volunteers needed:** Several. Will depend on the number of activities and participants.

**How/Notes:**
- Select the venue
- Select the decorations and activities
- Have fun!

Possible activities:
- Read beach stories
- Talk about famous beaches or things to do at the beach
- Decorate sugar cookies
- Limbo contest
- Sandwich making party
- Beach BINGO (cards with cute beach things)
- Decorate flip-flops(Program #52) or foam sunglasses
- Beach ball volleyball

# #21 – Combination craft & community service – Plastic bag pom-pom's and clothing drive/exchange

Sound strange? The concept is simple, the execution unexpected. Ask patrons to bring in either clothing to donate or plastic grocery sacks, or clothing to donate IN plastic grocery sacks. The program will use both, includes exercise and will be lots of fun. This is a very good community bonding activity.

**Target Audience:** Children & families

**Things needed:**
- Plastic bags
- Donated clothes
- Rubber bands or string
- Scissors – several pairs
- Colored ribbon (optional)
- Painter's tape
- Timer & whistle (optional)
- Prizes (small, like tattoos or pencils)
- A clear table for arranging clothes
- Extra plastic bags
- Cold water and/or juice

**Prep Time:** Need to arrange a fairly large open space for the game and have crafting space for the pom-poms

**Program Time:** 1 – 1 ½ hours

**Number of Participants:** Limited only by space and fire code

**Number of Friends/Volunteers needed:** At least 2

**How/Notes:** Do this program about a month before school starts. The pom-poms will help rev everyone up for the start of school. The clothing exchange will help off-set the cost of outfitting growing kids.

To make the pom-poms:

- Fold the bag so that the sides are tucked in, then fold into thirds lengthwise.
- Cut about an inch off the bottom finished edge and cut off the top handles
- Lay out the bottom piece and fold the bag over top of it (like the bottom edge is a towel rack) and the bag is laying over it.
- Use the scissors to make small cuts up to the "line" (the bottom edge piece) So, like you are cutting the towel, but not the rack.
- Lay over some ribbon too, if using
- Tie a tight knot with the bottom edge piece (the towel rack), then use the remaining over-hang to make a handle.
- Use fingers to work the fringe pieces open so that they are fluffy like pom-poms.

Many communities have gone away from plastic bags, so if plastic is no longer available in the community, substitute clean rags. If clean rags are used, cut into thin strips and tie in half.

Use the pom-poms to cheer on the team in the game.

Donated clothes will be used to play a game called "Clean your room." Divide everyone into teams (make sure teams are of a size proportionate to the size of the game space) and throw out an equal number of clothes onto each side. Use the painter's tape to put down a center line. Don't worry; the clothes won't be damaged any more than they already have been by lying around on bedroom floors.

On the GO signal, each side tries to 'clean their room' by throwing their clothes into the other room (other side's space)

Random finish times and a "no holding on to clothes" rule keeps the game very fast-paced and fun. No one will even realize they are exercising!

After everyone has had a chance to play a few times, lay out the clothes by size and gender while game participants enjoy a cold drink and talk about how much fun they just had.

Give out fresh bags and allow everyone to shop for a few items that might fit their needs. Theoretically participants should take only as many items as they brought in, but it doesn't always work like that. If there is a problem, or potential problem, consider issuing tickets for number of items allowed based on the number of items donated. Of course, other participants who donate might not find items they can use, so the leftovers should be donated to a local thrift store.

Warning! This activity is so much fun; it may make the regular rotation of programs.

# #22 – Parachute play

My young nieces love, LOVE playing with a big parachute. There are so many activities that can sneak in learning, that the participants in this program will have no idea that it is (shhh!) educational.

**Target Audience:** 2-6 year olds

**Things needed:**
- An enthusiastic Facilitator
- A nylon parachute
- Games to play
- Music (optional)

**Prep Time:** Minimal to arrange a space large enough to accommodate the parachute and jumping children

**Program Time:** 45 minutes to an hour

**Number of Participants:** Depends on the size of the parachute. 6-10 is optimum, so registration is recommended.

**Number of Friends/Volunteers needed:** 1-2

**How/Notes:** Skills enhanced – listening, teamwork, exercise
Some games:
- Mushroom:  On the count of three, all children holding the parachute lift it over their heads and pull it behind them. They then sit down on the edge of the parachute, which makes it look like a mushroom cap.
- Popcorn: Place any number of beanbags or lightweight balls on the parachute. The children then shake the parachute, making the beanbags or balls pop like popcorn.
- Sharks: All participants sit on the ground and pull the parachute toward their chest, keeping their legs underneath it. One or two children crawl around under the parachute, pretending to be sharks. They quietly grab the legs of

children holding the parachute and pull them under. Be prepared for lots of delighted screams with this game.

- Waves: While holding the parachute in both hands, children move their arms up and down to make small and large waves.
- One-Hand Run: Have children turn to one side, holding the parachute in one hand. On the start cue, they run (or skip or hop) in the same direction, causing the parachute to go around and around. After a few minutes or set number of rotations, try changing direction.
- The Flying Parachute: On the start signal, all participants swing the parachute upward, trying to keep it in the air for as long as possible.
- Fruit Salad: Give each child the name of a fruit, such as apple, strawberry or pear. When you call out the name of a fruit, everyone with that fruit name changes places by running under the parachute. When you yell "Fruit Salad!" everyone must swap places with the players on the other side.
- Rollerball: Place a ball on the parachute. The goal is to keep the ball moving only along the edge of the parachute by raising it as the ball approaches and lowering it as the ball rolls past. Try this with a football for an extra challenge.

Wind down with a story, and cold water.

# #23 – Count down to noon – New Year's Eve celebration

What does New Year's Eve mean? To grown-ups it is a time to reflect on the previous year and celebrate the beginning of the new. For young people though, the concept of the passing of another year is a bit big for some of them to wrap their brains around. Instead of trying to teach it, just celebrate it like they may have seen in the movies or on television.

**Target Audience:** Young children and families

**Things needed:**
- A big clock with a second hand
- Party supplies (see How/Notes)
- Count down numbers (use regular paper with the numbers 10, 9, 8... printed as large as possible. Make one that says HAPPY NEW YEAR! too)
- Sparkly juice
- Snacks
- Noisemakers or poppers (purchase some or make some at the party)
- Stories
- Face Painting (optional)
- Tattoos (optional)
- Supplies to make a memory book (pre-printed paper, staples, markers and crayons – See How/Notes)
- The library's resources on the subject

**Prep Time:** Will depend on how elaborate the party

**Program Time:** 1 ½ - 2 hours

**Number of Participants:** Limited only by space and fire code

**Number of Friends/Volunteers needed:** Several – will depend on the activities chosen

**How/Notes:** Party supply thoughts:

- A big Styrofoam ball and squares of aluminum foil. Participants can pin or tape them on to make a sparkly ball drop together. Make sure to have a flashlight to shine on it when the time comes!
- The memory book:
  - Take four 8 ½ x 11 inch sheets of paper and print questions on them so that when they are cut into 8 ½ x 5 ½ inch sheets, there will be a question at the top of each sheet. Consider a colored sheet for the cover (20__ Memories) and back page (Next year I want to____)
  - Other possible questions: At the end of 20__, my favorite:
    - Food is
    - Friend is
    - Game is
    - Place to go is
    - Toy is
    - Song is
    - Book is
    - TV show is
  - Stack the sheets together, then staple on the left. Write instructions to draw pictures to accompany the answers written in the book
  - Make this a station at the party.

Have a story time a few minutes before the big countdown.

After story time, hand out the noisemakers and/or poppers.

Line up 11 participants and give them each a countdown number. Instruct them to hold their number up over their heads when their number is called. The last one in the line should have the sign that says HAPPY NEW YEAR!

This would also be a great time to give a "Year in Review" of library patronage, circulation statistics and programming.

It is also a good time to take an interest poll of programming ideas for the upcoming year. Do this at the last few programs of the year to get feedback from a wider spectrum of patrons. Or, run it all of December depending on the traffic numbers.

*"There are many ways to enlarge your child's world. Love of books is the best of all." Jacqueline Kennedy*

# #24 – Teacher Thank-You letters

Teacher Appreciation Week is the second week in May. For this program, the main goal is to get students into the library. Have some Summer Reading material available, maybe even the registration forms, and provide grade level reading lists. Chat participants up as they make cards to thank their teachers for all their hard work.

**Target Audience:** School aged children, especially elementary kids

**Things needed:** Card making supplies
- Card stock
- Markers
- Contrasting papers
- Construction paper
- Stickers
- Glue & glitter (your choice – can be quite messy)
- Inspirational sayings such as, "Thanks for helping me grow" on a flower cut-out, or "You rule!" on a ruler.

**Prep Time:** Approximately ½ hour to set-up the area. Make sure to have plenty of flat spaces for creation.

**Program Time:** Recommend this be a drop-in program run for a few hours. That way, many patrons can participate, but they won't all be on top of each other.

**Number of Participants:** Limited only by supplies

**Number of Friends/Volunteers needed:** 1-2

**How/Notes:** Consider tying this program in with the Cookies in a Jar (Program #18) or Terrariums (Program #16) to make a nice gift for a special teacher. If one of these ideas is incorporated into the program, registration will be recommended, or a notice that supplies are limited will need to be included in the advertising.

# #25 – Paper airplane workshop

I'm guessing that nearly every American at some point in their life, will make a paper airplane and experience the joy of watching it soar. At the old Kingdome in Seattle, event goers used to play a game during events. From the top tier folks would launch a paper airplane in an attempt to land it on the field. It didn't happen often, but when it did, the crowd erupted! Incorporate some fun skill challenges into this program to take it up a notch. Celebrate National Paper Airplane Day on May 26th and kick off a great summer.

**Target Audience:** Young children and families

**Things needed:**
- An Instructor/Facilitator
- Samples
- Instruction sheets
- Paper
- Markers
- Scissors
- Paper clips or other small weights (monitor closely because these are choking hazards for small children)
- Appropriate material for skill games (See How/Notes)

**Prep Time:** ½ hour to lay out supplies and set up games

**Program Time:** 1 – 1 ½ hours

**Number of Participants:** Registration recommended. Recommend limiting this program to 20 or less unless an outside location is available, in which case, the sky's the limit.

**Number of Friends/Volunteers needed:** 2, including Instructor/Facilitator

**How/Notes:** Assign numbers to each plane and note who is assigned each number.

Possible games:

- Closest to the mark – Use a hula hoop as a target – whoever is closest wins.
- Distance – whose plane will go the farthest?
- Target practice – set up targets and see who can hit them.
- Post the results on a board at the circulation desk for a week or so to generate interest for the next time the program is run.

Resources:

*http://www.10PaperAirPlanes.com*
*http://www.instructables.com*

# #26 – Fancy Nancy tea party with tiara making

Beautiful tables, fancy finger sandwiches, plastic tea cups while enjoying Fancy Nancy stories – what could be better? A tiara, of course! Start this program with tiara making and finish with a fun tea party and the young Fancy Nancy lovers will have a fine time!

**Target Audience:** 3-9 year olds

**Things needed:**
- "Fancy Stuff" (Recommend discount or second-hand stores for feather boas, tablecloths (I think Fancy Nancy is fond of pink and purple), beads, and plastic teacups
- Tiara making supplies – a template, glitter pens, stickers, glue, jewels
- Fancy music
- Sandwiches (kid friendly, but beware of allergies)
- Plates & napkins
- Fancy Nancy books

**Prep Time:** About ½ hour for set-up, plus shopping

**Program Time:** 1½ -2 hours

**Number of Participants:** Registration required. Recommend less than 20 to keep things intimately "fancy." Include a question about food allergies on the registration form.

**Number of Friends/Volunteers needed:** At least 2 fancy helpers

**How/Notes:** Start things off as participants arrive with the tiara making activity. As they finish they can dance a bit. Then have a few stories and talk about how Fancy Nancy might handle a few sticky (age appropriate) situations. Finish the program with the fancy tea party.

# #27 - Puppet show

Kids love puppet shows. However, a puppet show, done poorly, can really turn them off. Make the most of this opportunity and grab hold of the youngest patrons with a great show of a classic story.

**Target Audience:** 0-9 year olds

**Things needed:**
- Puppeteers and "stage"
- A contract
- Chairs for grown-ups (line the space with chairs, which corrals the children and the adults can still see)
- A blanket (or several) for the floor (optional or encourage patrons to bring their own)
- Snacks (optional)
- A larger venue to accommodate more children (if needed)

**Prep Time:** If a professional is hired, the prep time will only consist of preparing the presentation space, making and distributing a flyer. If the high school drama club or any other amateur group is used, recommend previewing the presentation to ensure it is right for the intended audience.

**Program Time:** Plan on a run-time of 1 hour for a puppet show program. A few minutes to introduce, about 30 minutes for the program and about 20-25 minutes for questions and demonstration. Hopefully, the puppeteer will have time for questions and to show how the puppets work.

**Number of Participants:** Only limited by the fire code of the venue

**Number of Friends/Volunteers needed:** 1-2

**How/Notes:** Recommend that consideration be given to the high school drama club if there is one, or hiring a professional. And, stick with a classic story so that the focus stays on the puppets.

A puppet show requires little of the Friends other than advertising and to have a representative present during the event to introduce the show and to clean up afterwards.

Several months prior –

- Decide the desired show (can be used to kick-off Summer Reading, Summer reading culmination, cultural celebration or festival in town, or stand-alone)
- Hire the puppeteer. Most professional puppeteers have a catalog of shows to choose from, or talk with the Drama Club and brainstorm ideas. If the Drama Club is used, they may need some supplies purchased, so be prepared to support their needs.
- Get a venue. If the library is large enough, great. Otherwise, look to the closest elementary school or other public venue for support.
- Once the date and show are chosen, put the program on the library & community calendars.
- Email the flyer to subscriber the list for the age group, as well as, day-care providers and elementary schools in the area.

This program needs a back-up plan. Anything can happen, especially if the performer is traveling from far away.

# #28 – Planes, trains, automobiles & more – Trip planning for going on the road with kids

"Getting there is half the fun." Ever heard that phrase? Sometimes that is true and sometimes it is decidedly NOT! Whether the trip is a few hours or several days, heading out for a family vacation can be exhausting, frustrating, and so full of fun that the family will talk about it for years to come. Good planning will go a long way in ensuring a memorable journey. Get the kids involved in this one, it is their trip too. Couple this program with the Make & take road trip box (Program #29) for a home run!

**Target Audience:** Families

**Things needed:**
- A Presenter/Facilitator
- A matrix for families to fill in
- A list of age appropriate and transportation mode activities for traveling
- Audiovisual support (if needed)

**Prep Time:** About ½ hour to arrange space

**Program Time:** 1 hour – approximately 30 minutes to introduce the topic and take questions, then 30 minutes for families to work.

**Number of Participants:** Limited only by space and fire code, however, families will need to spread out to do their planning, so take that into consideration. Registration may be required.

**Number of Friends/Volunteers needed:** 2 (the Presenter/Facilitator and a helper)

**How/Notes:** Remind participants to keep expectations realistic. The vision of parents of a vacation full of good times, glorious wide-eyed and curious children who are remarkably well-behaved only happens in dreams!

Break the trip down into segments. Depending on the ages of the children traveling, snacks and rest breaks will need to be factored in.

Make sure some of the activities chosen involve either getting out the car (or seat if traveling by plane or train or boat).

Assign an Activities Coordinator – Put a child in charge of a portion of the trip. For short trips, one child takes charge of getting there and the other one plans the trip back. Break up longer trips based on what works for the trip, mode of transportation, and family.
The list of possible activities:

- The Alphabet Game: Everyone takes turns looking for letters on road signs and billboards, starting with the letter A and making their way through the alphabet. You can do this as a competition or as a group activity.

- The Picnic Game: The first person says, "I'm going on a picnic and I'm bringing an apple" (or anything starting with A). The next person continues with B but must also remember what A was and so on until someone brings a zebra (or something starting with a Z). Note: You almost never get to Z, but it is a fun game that everyone can play and works for all modes of transportation.

- The License-Plate Game: Players try to spot license plates from as many states as they can. Whoever spots the most states wins. Someone should be in charge of keeping track.

- 20 Questions: One person thinks of a person or a thing, and the others take turns asking questions to guess who or what it is. Questions must be answered only by "yes" or "no." For little kids, use family members and friends or familiar objects.

- Name That Tune: Hum nursery rhymes for the younger kids or pop songs for older ones. Or try turning the radio or CD player on for a few seconds and see who can guess the song the fastest.

- The Question Game: Ask open-ended questions such as "If you won a million dollars, what would you do with it?" "If you could pick only one food to eat forever, what would it be?"
- The Animal Game: One person thinks of an animal, and others take turns asking questions to guess what animal it could be.
- Letterboxing (Program #118)
- I Spy: The "spy" says "I spy something with my little eye that is (filling the blank with a color)." Another version is to say "something that starts with the letter A." Then, everyone else guesses what it is. To keep the noise down, it may be necessary to take turns. This is not the best car game, as things spied may be long gone by the time anyone can guess.
- Tid-bits about the destination. Really fun if the destination is to be a surprise.
- Bingo: There are plenty of printables online for different modes of travel.
- Hangman: word guessing game. Not suitable for driver participation, but great for the plane or back seat.
- Coloring books and/or sticker books
- Write a story together
- Name every single thing you can think of that starts with a letter, or is a certain color, or is associated with a certain thing (like the ocean).
- 10 things I like about you: Everyone takes turns providing something they like about each of their traveling companions.
- Songs: Find a classic road song or write a song together.
- Travel size board games (which usually have magnets)
- Paper dolls
- Audio books
- Write Life Lists together (Program #117)
- DEAR time: Drop everything and read. Not suitable for driver participation, but great for the plane or back seat.
- Story cubes: Roll the dice and make up a story

- Mad Libs®
- Find funky diners or unique museums
- Rest stop round robin: These are activities to get the blood flowing to satisfy what my son used to say, "I have jumping inside me that needs to get out!"
  - Frisbee
  - Jump rope
  - Kite-flying
  - Calisthenics circuit – one minute jumping jacks, one minute run in place, one minute windmills

The premise of the program is to encourage patrons to give more thoughtful consideration to the journey, along with the destination, and truly make getting there half the fun.

Make a fillable matrix like the one below for families to fill in.
SAMPLE:
**Trip Name:** Grandma & Grandpa's for the weekend
**Trip Length:** 4 hours
**Planned Stops:** Rest Stop – 50 miles, Lunch, Rest Stop after lunch

| Time | Activity | Activity Coordinator |
|---|---|---|
| Up to rest stop | Mad Libs and 10 things I love about Grandma & Grandpa | Zoe |
| At rest stop | Jump rope | Jaine |
| Up to lunch | Audio book | Mom's choice – it's a surprise! |
| Up to rest stop | Travel BINGO | Jaine |
| Rest stop | Kite flying | Zoe |

# #29 – Craft – Make & take road trip box

"I'm bored!" "How much longer?" These excessive questions are less of a problem when you've been to the library & picked up a few books on your intended destination, and put together a road trip box. This program/project would be great teamed up with a presentation of the movie classic "Family Vacation" starring Chevy Chase. The best time of year for this program is May – June.

**Target Audience:** Children and families

**Things needed:**
- Boxes (Recommend plain photo boxes for this project)
- Fun Road trip materials (Disposable camera (one per box), Mini journals, coloring sheets, Mad Libs®, Coloring Books, Travel Bingo, Scavenger Hunt Sheets)
- Decorating materials for the boxes (stickers, markers, jewels, glue)

**Prep Time:** ½ hour to lay everything out plus shopping.

**Program Time:** About 30 minutes to an hour, or 2½ hours if showing a movie too. If not showing a movie, it could be presented as a drop-in, "while supplies last" program.

**Number of Participants:** Limited by the number of supplies purchased. Recommend giving one box per family or per child and pre-registration for this program.

**Number of Friends/Volunteers needed:** 1-2

**How/Notes:** Consider coupling this program with the Planes, Trains, Automobiles & more – trip planning for going on the road with kids (Program #28) to up the excitement factor and help plan the box contents as well as, make a list of additional needs based on the activities chosen for the trip.
Road Trip Box –
*http://www.education.com/slideshow/printables-road-trip/*

# #30 – Fairy houses

Fairies have been delighting children for a very long time. And, building them a home to call their own is quite hospitable indeed. Compile some ideas, and lots of little supplies and have fun crafting fairy houses. This is also a good program to use up little bits of supplies left-over from other programs.

**Target Audience:** 4-11 year olds

**Things needed:**
- A Facilitator or two
- A few samples for inspiration
- Unfinished wooden bird houses, or empty oatmeal containers, empty milk jugs (very clean), or old bleach bottles (very, very clean) *Careful when using plastic containers. The cuts create very sharp edges, so think about covering rough edges with tape.
- Paint & paint brushes
- Glue
- Multi-sectioned trays or bowls to hold the fairy house adornments
- Flat trays for participants to "shop" the adornments, then take back to their worktables
- Fairy house adornments
    - Fluffy stuff (cotton balls, batting, wool, felt, cut up blankets)
    - Sticks, twigs & bark bits
    - Leaves
    - Stones
    - Wood bits (to craft chairs and tables)
    - Seeds and/or beans
    - Marbles
    - Sparkly things (sequins, gems, glass beads, old costume jewelry pieces)
    - Buttons
    - Feathers

- o  Silk or dried flowers
- o  Acorns or other nuts
- o  Moss
- o  Old doll house items (limit participants to one each)
- o  Ribbon
- o  Raffia
- o  Seashells
- o  Stickers
- o  Glitter
- o  Twine
- o  Markers

**Prep Time:** Approximately an hour to lay out all of the supplies

**Program Time:** By itself, this program can be done in an hour. If adding a movie or story, extend as needed.

**Number of Participants:** Recommend registration to ensure an adequate amount of supplies are available.

**Number of Friends/Volunteers needed:** At least 2

**How/Notes:**
Consider adding an activity to cover drying time; maybe a fairy movie or story.

# #31 – Leprechaun traps

As St. Patrick's Day nears, thoughts turn to a fun program to catch those sneaky, suspicious little leprechauns. Everyone knows that leprechauns love sparkles, so use a little sparkle bling-on-a-string to bait the trap. When the leprechaun picks up the beaded string, he'll pull the stick and the trap will fall on him. Because he is magic, he won't be trapped long though, he'll trade escape for chocolate gold! (Make sure parents know this) Leprechaun traps come in a wide array of types. Keep things simple for this program and encourage participants to embellish further at home and provide photos back to the library to display.

**Target Audience:** Children ages 4-10

**Things needed:**
- An Instructor/Facilitator
- A great leprechaun tale – also talk about why these tricksters need to be caught!
- Supplies (will depend on the type of trap chosen, but at least sparkly pony beads, string, stickers, glitter, tissue, wrapping or construction paper, craft sticks, markers and pens)
- Scissors & glue
- Irish music (optional, but recommended)
- The library's resources about St. Patrick's Day

**Prep Time:** Will depend on the type of trap chosen, but prep time is primarily dedicated to gathering supplies and arranging space, so it really doesn't take too long.

**Program Time:** An hour including a story time

**Number of Participants:** Limited only by space and supplies. Participants will need space to work, so registration may be required.

**Number of Friends/Volunteers needed:** 1-2, possibly more. Work on a 6:1 ratio, participants to volunteer helper.

**How/Notes:** Here are a few ideas:

Start with a paper bowl or open box and cover it with green tissue, wrapping or construction paper, then glue on glitter so it sparkles. Add stickers, shamrocks, a note saying "Gold here" or anything else that may draw the leprechaun close. Then, string together sparkly beads on a string as "bait" for the leprechaun. Tie the string of beads to a craft stick and prop up the bowl with the craft stick. At home find a low dark spot for the trap. How about making a small path of glittery paper to lead the leprechaun to the trap? When the leprechaun grabs the string of sparkly beads, the toothpick will move and the bowl will drop down. With any luck, a leprechaun will be trapped inside!

Or try this variety. The same concept, except the leprechaun will need to climb in to retrieve the prize. Use craft sticks to build the box. Craft sticks come in a variety of colors, so a rainbow colored box would add some flair. When the leprechaun grabs the beads, the lid will fall, trapping him inside.

# #32 – Create a sticky note "book"

This program is a quick, but creative craft that will appeal to children because it will make a great gift for someone special. It is easy and it will give them an opportunity to decorate a blank canvas, thereby expressing their individuality and style. What could be better than that?

**Target Audience:** Ages 5+

**Things needed:**
- Cardboard
- Decorative paper
- Glue sticks
- Scissors
- Decorations (stickers, markers, colored pencils, glitter glue, bits of ribbon, pom-poms)
- Packages of 3" square sticky note pads

**Prep Time:** The cardboard and papers will need to be pre-cut so that participants are just assembling. Then, on program day, ½ hour of prep time to lay everything out.

**Program Time:** It really only takes a few minutes to make these, so a ½ hour run time is plenty. Or, this program works well as a drop-in for a 2 hour window, or as a station at a larger event.

**Number of Participants:** If conducting as a stand-alone project, registration is suggested, as supplies will be limited.

**Number of Friends/Volunteers needed:** 1-2 to demo and provide supplies. Suggest the sticky note pad be issued at check-in.

**How/Notes:** These are fun to make, so there may be many requests to "do another." If there is plenty of cardboard and paper, but the sticky note supply runs out, it is ok! Let participants make the shells and they can supply their own notepads later. Make sure to give everyone a copy of the template so they can share with others.

Dimensions: 2 each pieces of cardboard 3 ¼" x 3 ¼", 1 each piece of cardboard ⅜" x 3 ¼" and 1 each piece of card stock or firm paper 8 ½" x 4 ⅝" and trimmed as shown.

To make the books:
- Glue the pieces of cardboard to the piece of card stock with the gaps as shown so that they can be wrapped by the card stock on each end and each side.
- Glue a sticky note pad to a piece of cardboard, and fold over.
- Decorate and give to someone special.

# #33 – Make & take – Light switch plates

The personal style touches that say "this is my space" help children feel ownership in their home and confidence in expressing themselves. This program is fun for everyone and kids will leave with a unique piece they made themselves.

**Target Audience:** 3-12 year olds

**Things needed:**
- White single light switch plates (Have a few doubles on-hand just in case)
- Permanent markers (Sharpie® works great and comes in a large variety of colors)
- Stickers
- Decoupage glaze (I can vouch for the effectiveness of Mod Podge®)
- Foam paint brushes
- Bags to take the project home in
- A few samples for inspiration

**Prep Time:** ½ hour to lay out supplies and arrange space

**Program Time:** This is a good drop-in program. Just lay out the supplies for a few hours.

**Number of Participants:** Limited only by supplies

**Number of Friends/Volunteers needed:** 1 to monitor and provide instructions

**How/Notes:** Allow at least 15 minutes of drying time before packaging to take home. This will give participants more time to browse for materials to check out!
Make sure the marker has dried before applying the decoupage glaze or the colors will smear and run. Apply only a thin layer of glaze or the drying time will increase.

# #34 – Craft – Shrinky Dinks®

Shrinky Dinks® came out when I was a kid in the 70's, sometime in the mystical, dark "olden" days, according to my children. A time when kids somehow survived the cruelty of living without video games and microwave ovens – dark days, indeed. But there was a bright shining spot, a beacon of joy – Shrinky Dinks®! It was so much fun to watch plastic creations curl and shrink in size and intensify in color. Decades later, Shrinky Dinks® are still entertaining kids. This program would be fun as a charm bracelet, necklace, magnet or key chain offering. Good timing for the program might be right in front of Mother's Day or Father's Day.

**Target Audience:** 4-10 year olds

**Things needed:**
- A few Facilitators (to help with cutting and to use the oven for participants)
- Shrinky Dinks®. These come in pre-printed and blank
- Colored pencils
- Scissors
- Jewelry findings, key-chains or magnets
- Glue
- A few toaster ovens (careful not to plug in too many in one place)
- Pliers (if using jewelry findings)

**Prep Time:** ½ hour to arrange space and lay out supplies

**Program Time:** An hour

**Number of Participants:** 15 or less is optimum, so registration is recommended

**Number of Friends/Volunteers needed:** 2 for up to 15 participants

**How/Notes:** If presenting this program to support Mother's Day or Father's Day, think about setting out a card making station and making envelopes in pretty paper. Envelope templates are easy to find online. Make a slim envelope to hold the finished Shrinky Dinks® project.

*"Anyone who thinks this world is without magic, hasn't been to a library." - Amy Dominy*

# #35 – Make and take instruments

Every generation has the same complaint. "Kids these days just aren't challenged enough. Why when I was a kid, we....." Heard that one before? Me too. Well, when I was a kid, we made instruments out of all kinds of stuff and had tons of fun, jammin' with our friends. This program will give children an opportunity to learn a bit about sound and how to create it using common things. This program can be done as a drop-in over a few hours, as a follow-on activity after story time, or as a station at a larger event, perhaps the Band Jam (Program #188).

**Target Audience:** Children ages 4-10

**Things needed:**
- An Instructor/Facilitator
- Supplies (will depend on the instruments chosen)
- Adequate space for participants to work
- Music (optional but recommended)

**Prep Time:** Will depend on instruments chosen. Some of the recommended instruments will require a bit of prep time.

**Program Time:** An hour

**Number of Participants:** Limited only by space and supplies. Recommend registration if an issue is anticipated.

**Number of Friends/Volunteers needed:** 1-2

**How/Notes:** Have a quick discussion about music and sound before starting. Finish the program off with a cool jam session.
Consider trying:
- A comb and waxed paper kazoo. Provide a new comb and waxed paper and show participants how to pull it tight and blow through it to make a kazoo sound.

- A Box Guitar. Take an old box (cereal, shoe, tissue), cut an oval hole in the middle, but slightly to one side (do this ahead of time). Have the participants slide 3-4 rubber bands around the box so that they go over the hole. Put a pencil under the bands and at the back end of the hole (this will hold up the rubber bands so they make more noise). Consider adding a paper towel roll to make it look more "guitar," then decorate.
- Coffee can drum. Use an aluminum or plastic coffee can with a plastic lid. Cut paper to go around the can to doll it up a bit. Cut a large square or circle of fabric (can be pre-cut), then put glue on the top of the lid and lay it down on the fabric. Put the lid back on the can and secure it with twine, ribbon or yarn. Provide decorations like stickers and markers for the drum base (the paper part). Add a couple of pencils and this drum is ready to rock!
- Wrist bells. Take 1" ribbon and cut some perpendicular slices into it to secure the bells (don't go all the way to the edges). Use various sized jingle or sleigh bells and thread smaller ribbon through them. Then secure several to the larger ribbon, tie onto participant's wrist and enjoy the jingly sounds!
- A pseudo-Didgeridoo. A didgeridoo is an Australian aboriginal instrument made from the branches of native trees. There are reportedly strict cultural traditions surrounding who is allowed to make and play these unique instruments. If there is a possibility that members of the community may be offended by offering this sound making device to children, skip it. Otherwise, this instrument can be made using either PVC pipe (make sure the ends are sanded well), or paper towel tubes taped together. Provide paper to cover and decorations to add. The sound is achieved by blowing into the tube.
- Plate maracas. Take 2 plates (either sturdy paper or pie tins), and decorate the "down side." Put a handful – to a few handfuls (depending on the size of the hand) of beans, unpopped popcorn or small pebbles inside one of the plates. Put the other plate on top so that the rims are sandwiched

together and there is a large open space inside. Secure the rims with glue and/or staples (I recommend both). ** This instrument could also be made with empty water bottles or tubular cardboard cans. Just make sure the openings are secured so that the tiny bits inside don't fall out.

*Libraries were full of ideas–perhaps the most dangerous and powerful of all weapons."*
*- Sarah J. Maas, Throne of Glass*

# #36 – Theme party

When an author is able to capture the attention of the upper elementary and middle school crowd, they become almost instant superstars. Plus, the marketing beyond the books makes them the envy of all other authors. Embrace the fanaticism and throw a party for the young patrons and let them show their love.

**Target Audience:** $3^{rd}$ – $8^{th}$ graders

**Things needed:** Will vary depending on the theme chosen, but for each theme:
- Decorations
- Music
- A creative activity
- Theme food
- Games
- Movie (optional)

**Prep Time:** 1-3 hours depending on the extent of the decorations, number of participants and activities chosen.

**Program Time:** 2-3 hours

**Number of Participants:** Limited only by space and fire code, however, registration should be considered if it seems that the number of participants will outnumber food and supplies.

**Number of Friends/Volunteers needed:** At least 2

**How/Notes:** Consider the following themes:

Harry Potter
- Food: Why, Butter Beer, of course! The recipe I found calls for ginger ale or cream soda and butterscotch syrup (ratio is 4 oz. of soda to 1 tablespoon syrup). Mix and serve over ice. Or Pumpkin juice (orange sherbet and ginger ale)

- Activity: Wand making
- Game: Care of magical creatures. Hide a picture of Harry's owl Hedwig somewhere in the library. First one to find it wins.

## Diary of a Wimpy Kid

- Food: Cheese, cheese and more cheese, as well as a few other kid foods
- Activity: Zoo wee mama! How about a game of picture charades?
- Game: Best drawing contest or Pictionary® with a white board

## American Girl

- Food: Tea party sandwiches and "tea" (apple juice)
- Activity: Participants make bracelets or necklaces for themselves and their dolls
- Game: The American Girl series is based on a girl from different time periods, so consider games from the time period of a book. For example: Samantha is from the Victorian era so, how about practicing balancing books on heads and the last one to still have the book balanced is the winner?

## Laura Ingalls Wilder

- Food: Syrup cakes
- Activity: Corn cob doll making or churning butter or beeswax candle making
- Game: square-dancing

*"You see, I don't believe that libraries should be drab places where people sit in silence, that has been the main reason for our policy of employing wild animals as librarians." - Graham Chapman*

# Chapter 3 – Tweens through Teens

One word – Ownership. Without a sense of ownership, tweens and teens will not invest in the library. I cannot state emphatically enough the value of a Teen Council (aka Teen Advisory Board, Teen Advisory Group) for the library. The creativity, imagination and drive of young people truly is unparalleled; all they need is a chance to show what they can do to support the library and community. If the community isn't large enough to support a full Teen Council, then ensure that at a minimum, at least one or two teens are invited to represent the teen community interests by serving as advisors on the Friends of the Library Board.

Start with Vision and Mission statements for the group (See Chapter 1 for more information about Vision and Mission statements). The bottom line for the Vision and Mission statements is that the members of the Teen Council will need to know and understand the goals of the group. Once understood, they can then use the statements as a filter for decision-making throughout the year. You should hear statements like this in the meetings: "Our focus this year is on outreach and building the teen collection. Will funding new furniture fit into that?"

Revisit the documents annually, or sooner if needed (major changes to the community or library may push a look sooner than planned), and re-adjust the statements as the needs, interests and capabilities of the group change. Perhaps the Vision statement will be very broad and will not need to be changed, but the Mission statement (the how-we-get-there piece) will adjust from year to year.

Some sample Vision & Mission statements:
- **Vision:** We want to increase library patronage and circulation numbers through our efforts. **Mission:** To increase library usage and material check-out through

outreach programs and vibrant materials displays, book reviews and clubs, and social media "blitzes."

- **Vision:** We want an engaging space for teens to feel comfortable communicating with each other and doing homework at the library. **Mission:** To raise money to fund more, art pieces, furniture and redecorating of the Young Adult section.
- **Vision:** We want new ideas and entertainment presented in the library. **Mission:** To develop and support library programs for everyone throughout the year with an infusion of youth ideas, knowledge, talents, and volunteerism.

Next, members are needed. But, how do you appeal to teens who have school, other activities, jobs and friends on their plates already? Lay out what is needed or available based on their interests. Break down potential involvement like this:

## There are opportunities on Teen Council for:

Creative Types:
- Make & sell items to benefit/fund your ideas or programs
- Make displays, posters or bookmarks for the library
- Write a play, mystery or song to be performed at the library
- Write a teen newsletter for the library
- Decorate the library's Young Adult section
- Design advertising for programs

Performers:
- Give library tours
- Write & record a Public Service Announcement for the library
- Facilitate a book discussion or brainstorming session
- Read stories to children
- Greet, usher and help out at library programs

Tech-savvy Types:
- Design/update the library's webpage
- Manage social media posts
- Set up text alerts or listservs for programs
- Design a registration form for programs
- Write, shoot and produce a TV commercial for the Teen Council and/or library
- Teach the eReader or beginning computer classes

Planners/Helpers:
- Participate in brain-storming sessions
- Gather and analyze survey data
- Rearrange books, shelves and furniture in the library
- Set-up/clean-up library programs
- Choose new materials for the collection
- Assist with mailings or other big projects

And, that is just for starters! But, how do you get the word out about the Teen Council? Try:
- Posters to hang up at school
- Participation in local parades (Program #179)
- Starting a social media page and inviting teens to join
- Soliciting support while promoting Summer Reading Programs
- Make bookmarks with meeting information and distribute to school library and at circulation desk
- Flash/Freeze Mob at the mall with flyer distribution
- Local media plea
- Invite patrons who are coming to other library programs or seem to be in the library quite a bit
- Set up a 'Friend of a Friend' party at the library for current Teen Council members

# Council duties, membership and conduct

Next tackle the duties of those on the Council. What will they do based on the mission? Sample duties include, but are in no way limited to:

- Provide input for programming
- Recommend materials for purchase and addition to the collection
- Support library programs and fundraising events
- Participate in outreach programs
- Attend meetings
- Recruit
- Serve as a liaison between the library and other civic organizations partners

Will there be an application process? Do teens have to formally apply to the Council or can they just drop-in? Is there a maximum number of people who can be on the Council? Are there "officer" positions? Formality provides structure to the group, but may be a turn-off to potential members. Be flexible and build the group based on what feels right.

No matter how the group is structured, basic rules or bylaws will need to be in place to tackle any potential or perceived discord. Establish a Code of Conduct that everyone agrees to and abides by. Make sure parents are aware of their teen's involvement and agree to the terms of the group too.

What is the key to a successful Teen Council? It is several things:

- Meet regularly – set a timeframe for meetings and don't monkey with it for at least a year. If meeting times or frequency need to be adjusted after a year, do so, but let the Teen Council decide what is needed.
- Feedback – Solicit and respond to feedback from Teen Council members and other teens who use the library for services.

- Listen & Follow-up – If feedback is received, follow-up with information back on what is being done and its impact on teens and the library as a whole.
- Support & Respect – Show the teens involved in the Teen Council that their work is important by supporting their efforts and respecting their ideas. There is a good reason a Teen Council is a stand-alone organization – their needs are unique to them. Make sure to honor and embrace them!

Programs that Teens, along with their Tween friends may like:

*"A library is a place where you learn what teachers were afraid to teach you."* - *Alan M. Dershowitz*

# #37 – Job preparedness series

What does it take to get a job? Finding out who is hiring, or canvassing an area asking. Then, filling out an application – sometimes online, sometimes by hand. Preparing a winning resume. Creating a tracking system for applications. Preparing for, and dazzling during, the interview. Accepting a job and possibly negotiating a salary. Having all of the information needed for a job application and presenting a winning resume sets teens who attend this program well on their way to their first paycheck.

**Target Audience:** Teens

**Things needed:**
- An Instructor/Facilitator – Look to the Chamber of Commerce or Rotary President or someone who has been involved in Jr. Achievement for support.
- Tips on putting together a resume (discuss paper (weight and color), font, length, content)
- Computers to work on
- Some role-playing scenarios

**Prep Time:** Minimal onsite. Preparation is dedicated to preparing a tip sheet and scenarios

**Program Time:** 1 – 1 ½ hours

**Number of Participants:** Limit to the number of computers available.

**Number of Friends/Volunteers needed:** 1

**How/Notes:** Timing for this program should be in the April timeframe. Employers are starting to formulate their summer hire needs. Let the Chamber of Commerce know about the workshops and some companies may request to come and recruit.

Recommend running this as a series over 3-4 weeks, then repeating as needed, possibly in front of the winter holidays when employers take on seasonal employees.

Remind participants that when filling out a job application, neatness definitely counts. In fact, many employers are purposely avoiding the online application, because they want to see the handwriting and grammar skills of potential employees.

Make sure email is discussed. Email addresses should be professional and devoid of vulgarity. Someone who includes an unprofessional email address may lose out before they are even considered.

Dress standards. Applicants are judged during the interview, but also when they walk in the door to request an application. No matter what the job being sought, applicants should look clean and well put together from start to finish.

Discuss items that should and should not be included on a resume. How far back is relevant? How to put together a resume when you've never had a job. Are church activities okay to include? Should applicants have more than one resume?

Discuss a tracking system for the resumes sent out, or places applications were submitted. Who should they expect to hear from for each job, and when?

Preparing for an interview. The importance of familiarizing oneself with the company and the work environment cannot be overstated. Having a sense of what they do at the company will give the applicant the tools they need to ask questions appropriate to the employer. Preparation also allows for some role-playing and how to answer tough questions.

# #38 – Creative writing workshops

Teens have something to say and writing is an excellent venue for expressing thoughts. They are largely less encumbered than adults about expressing their imaginative thoughts, which is fantastic. Embrace their creativity by helping them hone the craft of writing.

**Target Audience:** Teens

**Things needed:**
- An Instructor/Facilitator
- Space to write
- Low music (optional)
- Pens & paper
- Writing prompts and exercises (optional but recommended)

**Prep Time:** Minimal to arrange space

**Program Time:** 1 hour

**Number of Participants:** Keep the group small, preferably less than 12, so registration is recommended.

**Number of Friends/Volunteers needed:** No additional volunteers are needed. The Instructor/Facilitator can handle this program.

**How/Notes:** It is best to establish a calendar with topics that will be covered. The program may morph over time, as many teen programs do, so be prepared to adapt as needed.
Possible topics:
- Character and plot development
- Voice
- Setting
- Endings
- Genre exploration
- Believability

# #39 – College readiness series

Applications, scholarships and grants – oh my! The process of getting a student into college, especially the first one, can be daunting. Wouldn't it be nice if there were local "veterans" who could be on-hand to assist in navigating the whole sea of the unknown... the college selection, application and attendance process? This program series will give parents/guardians and students all the available information on the topic and break it down into manageable pieces. Recommend this program be broken into an on-going series starting at the beginning of the school year and running monthly throughout the school year.

**Target Audience:** Teens and their parents/guardians

**Things needed:**
- Presenters – look for volunteers who have been through this process before. The high school guidance counselor is also an excellent option.
- Audiovisual support (if needed)
- A list of resources for each topic presented
- Snacks (optional)

**Prep Time:** Less than ½ hour to arrange space and set up audiovisual support

**Program Time:** 1 – 1 ½ hours

**Number of Participants:** Limited only by space, fire code, and Presenter preference. Some sessions may be "hands-on" in which case it is possible that fewer participants could be accommodated.

**Number of Friends/Volunteers needed:** 1-2 including the Presenter

**How/Notes:** Everything is a new experience and could be done as a program on their own: the SAT/ACT, choosing a school, knowing when to apply, getting scholarship and grant information, arranging school visits, weighing options when accepted to more than one school, trade-school options etc. etc. etc.

Make sure to include the value of college preparatory classes and exams and study tips too. How about adding these things too?

- A basic life skills lesson about things that many parents either haven't prepared their kids for, or assume that they already know, such as: laundry, ironing, balancing a checkbook, understanding a lease.
- Dorm life – etiquette, conflict resolution with roommates and finding time and space to study.
- Pitfalls – Avoiding the "Freshman 15," keeping a healthy immune system while everyone else seems to be getting sick, the party scene.

# #40 – Hair braiding

My daughter attends a summer camp program and one of the staff likes to braid hair. Different braids, different doo-dads, clippees etc. and my girl loves to show off a new "do" when she gets one. She just shines! I asked her one day if she would be interested in learning how to do these braids herself. Ding! Inspiration for another awesome library program.

**Target Audience:** 9-16 year olds

**Things needed:**
- An Instructor
- A model
- Hair accessories (bands, clips, bobby pins)
- Some music for practice time
- Hand mirrors
- Overhead mirror (if available)
- Combs and brushes (participants can bring their own or Friends can provide)
- Visual "cheat sheet" of the braids demonstrated

**Prep Time:** Minimal to arrange space and layout supplies

**Program Time:** An hour

**Number of Participants:** Fewer than 20 would be good, under 15, ideal, so registration is recommended. This program will likely fill up fast!

**Number of Friends/Volunteers needed:** 1 to facilitate + Instructor

**How/Notes:** Participants should be instructed to bring their own hairbrushes if they'd like, but the Friends should plan on providing some combs and a few extra accessories to add to the program.

The best way to do this is to have participants partner up.

The Instructor goes through a braid step by step while participants follow along.

Then switch! The braided becomes the braider and practices the same braid.

If each person gets about 10 minutes of practice time and the program is 1 hour, there should be enough time to learn 3 braids. Or, plan on two with the third as a bonus, or just extend the program to 1 ½ hours.

Small gift bags with the braiding "cheat sheets" and some hair accessories would add a very nice touch to this program.

# #41 – Zombie anything (or Vampires, Space Aliens, Wizards etc.)

Themed parties rock! Vampires, Aliens, Zombies – adapt as needed to embrace whatever pop culture obsession currently has grabbed the attention of the youth of the community. This is a great Teen Council program project. Let them do this as part of their year-end planning session, or just to bring their friends into the library.

**Target Audience:** Tweens to Teens

**Things needed:** Will depend on activities chosen (See How/Notes)
- Theme
- Fun advertising
- Decorations
- Food
- Music
- Games (supplies will depend on games chosen)

**Prep Time:** Will depend on activities chosen

**Program Time:** 2-3 hours

**Number of Participants:** Registration recommended to make sure there is enough food and supplies for everyone.

**Number of Friends/Volunteers needed:** At least 2

**How/Notes:**
Zombie Games:
- Who would win in a fight? Pit the pop culture star of the show up against other would-be adversaries. Example: Zombies vs. Aliens – Zombies of course! Because they are on home turf and the aliens don't know that the zombies are un-dead. Throw it out there and let participants give their thoughts.
- Board game called Last Night on Earth

- Zombie Survivor – A tag came like Sharks and Minnows where once tagged, the tagged person becomes a Zombie too. Last one not tagged is the winner. Twist this one and make everyone walk slow and stiff like Zombies.
- How about a costume contest?
- Zombie dance-off. Get the best "Thriller" moves out and dance it out.

And, speaking of music, here are some other suggestions:
- Nine inch nails – Dead Souls
- The Cranberries – Zombie
- The Doors – People are Strange
- Danny Elfman – Psycho
- Rob Zombie – House of 1000 corpses

Maybe a movie? These are good ones that aren't too disgusting:
- Cult classic – Night of the Living Dead
- Dawn of the Dead
- Zombieland

Use the same formula of games, movie and music for the other pop-culture genres listed.

# #42 – Sleepover at the library

I've always felt like I'm getting away with something if I'm somewhere "after hours" and the place is closed. It kind of adds to the mystique of the whole experience. A sleepover at the library should include lots of fun after-dark activities. Segregate for this one – boys get their own night and so do girls.

**Target Audience:** Tweens and Teens

**Things needed:**
- Activities
- Food (Breakfast (keep it simple) and snacks)
- Music
- Movies
- Flashlights for story-telling
- Parental consent and liability release form
- Conduct agreement

**Prep Time:** About an hour – more depending on activities planned

**Program Time:** Overnight – say 8 pm to 8 am

**Number of Participants:** Registration will be required for this event.

**Number of Friends/Volunteers needed:** At least 2 – the ratio will be determined by local policies.

**How/Notes:** Consider activities like Glow in the dark scavenger hunt (Program #57), Reader's theatre (Program #73), any of the make and take teen crafts, gaming tournament (Program #67)

Perhaps the event can be used as a brain-storming session for development of the programming plan for the upcoming year? There are a myriad of methods of determining the reliability of volunteers. Consult with the library staff for legal guidelines.

# #43 – Film making workshop

Ever wonder how a movie actually gets made? I know I do, and teens do too. Take participants from idea to filming to editing to final product in this program that will require a team commitment over a period of time. Or, if a lesser commitment is needed or requested, break down the process into a several part series. I recommend considering tying the whole program into a submission for the Newbery Medal 90 second video contest. The details are listed at: *http://jameskennedy.com/90-second-newbery/*

**Target Audience:** Teens

**Things needed:**
- An Instructor/Facilitator/Production leader
- Video clips or video cameras to capture video
- Video editing software (there are several, so find one that the leader is familiar with and feels comfortable using)
- Storyboard
- Production space and time
- Audiovisual support

**Prep Time:** Time to formulate a plan, but arrangement requirements are minimal prior to the start.

**Program Time:** Will vary significantly depending on format.

**Number of Participants:** Will also depend upon format chosen. If doing an informational series, participants are only limited by space and fire code. If doing a Newbery 90 second video submission, participants should be limited to the number of actors and production staff needed.

**Number of Friends/Volunteers needed:** N/A – this program will be managed by the Production Leader or Instructor without additional Friend support unless requested.

**How/Notes:** Both the series and the 90 second Newbery video contest will be composed of the same elements:

- Types of film (narrative, documentary, experimental)
- A script or concept
- A storyboard
- Dialogue
- Character development
- Elements of cinematography (shot sizes, angles, exposure, depth)
- Production elements (pre-production – getting everything ready, production – shooting, post-production)
- Editing (fading, cutting, music overlay)

If the final product is a Newbery submission or public service announcement, find some way to stream it, whether it be on social media or an in-library demo/display.

# #44 – Moss graffiti

Graffiti is destructive, illegal, difficult to clean up, bad for the environment, and in many cases, beautiful. In gang laden areas, which is now nearly everywhere, graffiti tags are used to mark territory. Businesses spend large portions of their budgets combating and cleaning up after graffiti. So what does all of that have to do with the library, and more specifically moss graffiti? Moss graffiti is an eco-friendly, artful, fun alternative. The question is: would businesses be interested? If any of them are open to the idea, consider a moss graffiti program. Could the library start the trend? Go really hog-wild and make it a community-wide movement on a large scale which would be quite newsworthy. Or, if no one seems open to the idea, the project can still be taught and introduced with participants painting moss graffiti on paving stones and taking their creations home.

**Target Audience:** Teens

Things needed:
- An Instructor/Artist to introduce the idea, discuss mosses, graffiti and moss graffiti
- Audiovisual support requested by the Instructor/Artist (there are online video resources available to support introduction of the topic)
- Moss (3 handfuls per batch)
- Blender (or bucket and immersion blender)

- Sugar (1/2 teaspoon per batch)
- Buttermilk (2 cups per batch)
- Water (2 cups lukewarm per batch)
- Container with lid (for mixture)
- Smaller containers for participants
- Paint Brushes
- Spray bottles with water
- A wall – preferably brick or concrete, but moss will grow on almost anything
- Paving stones (if not using an outside space)

**Prep Time:** 30 – 45 minutes to arrange space and set up supplies

**Program Time:** Depends. If there is only a small space, or if using paving stones, the program could be completed in an hour. If the space available is larger and the recipe is duplicated, the project could go on for a few hours or days, depending on the scale and number of participants.

**Number of Participants:** Limited only by space and supplies

**Number of Friends/Volunteers needed:** 1-2

**How/Notes:**
>1. Clean the moss, then crumble it into a blender.
>2. Add in water, buttermilk, and sugar.
>3. Pulse the blender until the mixture forms a gel-like substance.
>4. Pour the mixture into a smaller containers and paint it onto a wall outside. Make sure to choose a wall that doesn't receive much sunlight, as most mosses grow best in shady areas.
>5. Mist the mossed wall or stone with water once a week and watch the creation grow!

# #45 – Red Cross babysitting class

Gaining confidence in taking care of children is a bit like trying to get a professional job after college. Employers want experience, but the applicant can't get experience without a job! In this case, graduates from the Red Cross babysitting class will have an "advanced degree" to offer parents. According to the Red Cross website, this class teaches students to:

- Care for babies and kids up to 10 years old
- Keep the kids and yourself safe
- Make playtime fun with age appropriate games
- Handle a wide variety of emergencies
- Manage your babysitting business

**Target Audience:** Tweens & Teens

**Things needed:**
As this is an established class and the library is only facilitating, all instructors and instruction materials will be provided by the Red Cross.

**Prep Time:** Minimal to arrange space

**Program Time:** Will depend on format chosen

**Number of Participants:** Will depend on the number of available computers and the budget

**Number of Friends/Volunteers needed:** 1

**How/Notes:** This class is offered two ways, online and in person. The online course is four hours, while the classroom version is six hours in length.

# #46 – Zentangle

Zentangle is an easy and fun art form. It looks difficult, but participants will soon be enjoying themselves as they see how simple it really is. Zentangle is an easy to learn and relaxing method of creating beautiful images from repetitive patterns created by Maria Thomas and Rick Roberts. They believe that "life is an art form and that Zentangle is a perfect metaphor for deliberate artistry in life." To learn more about the process, and for pattern ideas visit their beautiful web site at *www.zentangle.com*.

**Target Audience:** Tweens & Teens – Anyone interested

**Things needed:**
- Instructor/Facilitator
- Samples – for inspiration
- Quality paper
- Quality pens
- Colored pencils

**Prep Time:** Time to print and lay out some samples – approximately an hour.

**Program Time:** An hour

**Number of Participants:** Limited only by space and resources

**Number of Friends/Volunteers needed:** The Instructor/Facilitator can handle the whole program if there are less than a dozen participants. Ratio should be about 12:1

**How/Notes:** Take a look at *http://www.youtube.com* for ideas. Demonstrate and then let participants enjoy the fun and ease of Zentangle. Pull any library resources on the topic.

# #47 – Beginning car maintenance

Driver's Ed has changed. When I went through, basic car maintenance (checking fluid levels, troubleshooting, changing a tire etc.) was included. After a review of the National Highway Traffic Safety Administration standards, it appears that now basic services are no longer included in the driver's education curriculum. Some commercial companies may offer a block of instruction on maintenance and trouble-shooting, but new drivers really could use more information. Wouldn't it be nice if there was an expert available to show young drivers the vital skills of keeping their cars running properly? This program would be great as a series. I'd call it Bumper to Bumper – Car Maintenance for the Beginning Driver.

**Target Audience:** Beginning drivers

**Things needed:**
- An Instructor – solicit a volunteer from the community
- Enthusiastic new drivers or those on the cusp of getting a Learner's permit
- Audiovisual support (if needed)
- Library materials (show everyone where the Chilton manuals are in the reference section)

**Prep Time:** Minimal to arrange space

**Program Time:** An hour

**Number of Participants:** Recommend registration to keep the group small (less than 10).

**Number of Friends/Volunteers needed:** The Instructor can handle this program.

**How/Notes:** Cover the following as most drivers should be able to handle these things for themselves:
- Basic troubleshooting (the owner's manual stays in the car!)

- How to use jumper cables
- Checking fluid levels (oil, transmission, power steering, windshield wiper)
- Changing a tire
- Changing wiper blades
- Checking tire pressure and tread depth
- Filling a tire properly
- Benchmark services (oil, brakes, mileage)

# #48 – Business plans

I believe that enterprising teens would flock to the library for a program designed to help them get their business ideas off the ground. There are plenty of "business ideas" resources out there. All fine and good, but most of those resources encourage teens to "write a business plan and take action." This is where the teen stops reading because this whole project just became too hard. That glossy resource has tons of great ideas, but doesn't go the extra mile to explain what a business plan is, how to put one together, and what to do with the plan once it is done. Enter one awesome community leader, business owner or banker with the answers.

**Target Audience:** Teens

**Things needed:**
- A fantastic Presenter/Instructor with some sample templates
- Audiovisual support (if needed)

**Prep Time:** A few minutes – ½ hour depending on audiovisual requirements and whether snacks are provided or not.

**Program Time:** 1 ½ hours should suffice, but try to make sure the Presenter/Instructor is available for questions at the end, even if the program goes slightly over the scheduled time.

**Number of Participants:** Limited only by space and Presenter/Instructor's preference. Pre-registration recommended.

**Number of Friends/Volunteers needed:** 1

**How/Notes:** Consider a bulletin board in the library, on which teens can place advertisements for their business. Recommend prior approval of postings. Teens will get excited about their business/project and may forget something fundamental like, say, a phone number.

# #49 – Anime/Manga drawing discussion/demonstration

Anime is Japanese cartoon animation, and Manga is a Japanese drawing genre that is very popular among the 9-16 year old group. Pokemon, Baukugon, Yu-Gi-Oh!, and Dragon Ball Z are all examples of popular series produced using manga and anime.

**Target Audience:** 9-16 year olds

**Things needed:**
- An Instructor/Guide (look at the high school art department for assistance)
- All of the library's resources on this genre
- Audiovisual support (if needed)
- Drawing paper/pens/colored pencils/pencils/erasers
- An easel, white board or large drawing pad (if requested by the Instructor/Guide)
- Music (optional)
- Snacks (optional)

**Prep Time:** Minimal to set up table space and snacks, if offering.

**Program Time:** An hour

**Number of Participants:** Depends on the available space, but a small group (less than 10 is optimum) so that everyone gets personal instruction if desired. Registration recommended.

**Number of Friends/Volunteers needed:** This program can be managed by the Instructor/Guide. Add a volunteer if serving snacks.

**How/Notes:** This program may morph into a club, so gauge interest and be prepared to keep it going.

# #50 – "Up" cycling clothes

This trend, taking clothes and adding embellishments to either cover up flaws or stains or just bling them up, is a fabulous way for people to create something unique and truly individualized. "Fashion made for you, by you." Love it! Invite someone knowledgeable into the library to share their vision and methods with participants. Participants should be encouraged to bring in something of theirs that they'd like to up-cycle and wear as new, or donate to someone else. Be ready to be wowed by the creativity and laughter!

**Target Audience:** Tween & Teens

**Things needed:**
- An Instructor/Facilitator
- Some samples of items that have been transformed
- Audiovisual support (if needed)
- Sewing notions (needle, thread, scissors)
- A few sewing machines (optional but will open up the possibilities)
- An assortment of embellishments (ribbons, jewels, laces, buttons, iron-on transfers)
- Fabric glue
- Iron + ironing board
- Fabric paint (optional – Caution! Fabric paint, is paint. For. Fabric. If it gets on clothes, it won't come out, so be very careful)
- Shirts or blouses (participants should bring their own, but have a few extra on-hand in case someone forgets or messes up)
- Note-taking materials (optional)

**Prep Time:** About an hour to set up supplies and work tables

**Program Time:** Plan on 2 hours

**Number of Participants:** Depends on supplies available, as well as workspace. Registration recommended.

**Number of Friends/Volunteers needed:** 1 + Instructor/Facilitator

**How/Notes:** Ask participants to bring in an item of clothing that still fits, but has a stain, or a hole, or is simply in need of refreshing. Also make sure to have some extra clothes on hand for "cannibalizing" or upcycling in case someone doesn't bring in their own. Jeans with back pockets are great for this task.

As the ideas are discussed, participants will formulate ideas of what they'd like to do, so consider providing some note taking materials.

Facilitating the ideas will depend on the number of participants vs. the number of sewing machines. A waiting line for a sewing machine will reduce the fun factor, so encourage buttons, iron on pieces, jewel rivets and other things that can be done by hand. This will keep things moving.

# #51 – Make-up application

Around middle school is when girls start to get serious about regularly wearing make-up. Some sooner, some later, some boys, but for the most part, this program is aimed at middle school girls.

**Target Audience:** 11-14 year olds

**Things needed:**
- An Instructor/Facilitator
- Someone well versed in made-up application. It could be a salon owner, someone from the department store make-up counter, or a Mary Kay or Avon representative. Note: If a company representative is used, make sure they do not attempt to sell or specifically endorse their product. They can leave cards and use their products to demonstrate – just no selling on-site.
- A semi-private to private space
- Participants can be instructed to bring their own make-up if they'd like a color evaluation
- Disposable applicators (cotton swabs work well for this)
- Disposable cleaning cloths – like baby wipes (or use inexpensive washcloths)
- Hand mirrors, or lighted mirrors, or a combination
- Music (optional)
- Snacks (optional)

**Prep Time:** About ½ hour to set out snacks (if using), mirrors and disposable applicators.

**Program Time:** 1 – 1 ½ hours

**Number of Participants:** Recommend registration for this program. Participants should be less than 15.

**Number of Friends/Volunteers needed:** 1 + Instructor/Facilitator

**How/Notes:** Start with a discussion on the importance of a clean face, moisturizer with sunscreen – the sooner this lesson is learned, the better.

Discuss the differences between what is considered day and night make-up applications and the benefits of looking fresh vs. looking like a cartoon character. It would also be nice to include a discussion on the value of appreciating the natural beauty and beauty within a person (avoid sounding "preachy"). Make-up serves as an enhancement, not a mask.

If possible, conduct this program in natural light.

# #52 – Flip-flop decorating

Given the opportunity, I think my daughter would wear flip-flops 10 months out of the year. Personally, I never got used to the feel, but oh man! There are some cute DIY flip-flop ideas out there. Present a few ideas and let the crafty participants get to work.

**Target Audience:** Tweens and Teens

**Things needed:**
- An Instructor/Facilitator
- Some sample finished pieces
- Flip-flops (Recommend participants be asked to bring their own, but make sure to have a small assortment available for those who may forget)
- Decorations/Embellishments (Sequins, glitter, silk flowers, ribbon, craft foam)
- Glue gun
- Scissors
- T-shirts (Men's large) in a variety of colors

**Prep Time:** About ½ hour to arrange space and lay out supplies

**Program Time:** An hour

**Number of Participants:** Recommend registration to ensure there are ample supplies and everyone has adequate work space

**Number of Friends/Volunteers needed:** 2, including the Instructor/Facilitator

**How/Notes:** Here is one of my favorite, super simple ideas. Only scissors and an old t-shirt are required to doll-up the flip-flops.
1. Take an adult size large t-shirt and cut off the bottom hem. Then cut two strips of approximately 1" from the bottom. There should be enough to get eight strips from one shirt
2. Cut open.

3. Use finger to make the strip curled by running the thumbnail down the middle of the fabric.
4. Pass the fabric strip through the post of the flip-flop so that the middle of the fabric is at the post and it is on the foot side of the post and facing up (you should still be able to see the whole flip-flop).
5. Then, bring one of the strips over the top (right at the post) and thread through to the opposite side and under (right at the post).
6. Do the same thing from the other side and this should show the top of the flip-flop covered at the post.
7. Then, opening the fabric as you work, simply wrap each side with a slight overlap to the end where the flip-flop strap meets the sole mid-foot.
8. At this point work the fabric back up the strap about an inch to an inch and a half.
9. Slide the flip-flop onto the foot and bring the straps back to behind the heel and tie into a square knot. (This knot will stay permanently)
10. Bring the fabric to the front and tie a pretty bow
11. Embellish as desired

# #53 – Jewelry making

What is jewelry anyway? Jewelry is described as "an accessory to adorn the wearer to add style." Jewelry can be made from a variety of mediums which is great for teenagers, as they tend to love anything that will make them feel unique.

**Target Audience:** Tweens and Teens

**Things needed:**
- An Instructor/Facilitator
- Sample pieces
- Jewelry making supplies and findings for chosen project
- Trays to contain small pieces (egg cartons work great for this)
- Tools (wire cutters, pliers, scissors, needles)

**Prep Time:** Up to an hour to prepare projects. Some projects will require less prep time

**Program Time:** An hour

**Number of Participants:** Recommend registration and the number of participants be limited to a dozen or less. This will ensure that the Instructor can provide individual attention if needed and that the noise level remains "library appropriate."

**Number of Friends/Volunteers needed:** 1 + Instructor/Facilitator

**How/Notes:** Recommend consideration be given to conducting this program as a series. It will be popular and there are so many jewelry options.

Consider:
- Earrings
- Rings
- Bracelets

- Necklaces
- Bead-making
- Weaving
- Jewelry for "stuff" like handbags, belts, shoes and hats

This would be a great program for teens on the Teen Council to run. They should take into consideration the amount of time and cost of supplies.

Explore different mediums like wire, glass, leather, feather, fabric, and thread. Also cover different techniques such as braiding, knotting, weaving, and fusing. The project possibilities are limitless.

# #54 – Re-cycled jewelry

Tweens especially love things that are funky and unique, like them. Things they make themselves are even better. This program will get creativity and giggles flowing freely. Have plenty of material available and present several sample ideas to get things started. There are many online resources for ideas. On *http://www.spoonful.com*, I found a matchbox locket and a snack bag chain bracelet. There are also many variations of a paper clip necklace and paper bead projects, as well as, wire with rocks and miscellaneous small hardware items like springs, nuts & washers.

**Target Audience:** Tweens-Teens

**Things needed:**
- An Instructor/Facilitator – look for an older teen or local artist to help out
- A variety of material as outlined in the projects listed above
- Complementary jewelry making items like ribbon, glitter, sequins, beads, necklace cording and embroidery thread
- Jewelry findings (fasteners, clips, key rings etc.)
- Scissors
- Pliers
- Small containers to keep items separated (egg cartons work well and can be saved for other projects)
- Paper plates (optional – for participants to contain their project pieces)
- Music (optional but recommended)
- Snacks (optional)

**Prep Time:** Time is needed to gather materials, then ½ hour to set up materials and arrange the space.

**Program Time:** An hour

**Number of Participants:** Registration recommended, as less than 15 is ideal for this program.

**Number of Friends/Volunteers needed:** 1-2

**How/Notes:** The Instructor/Facilitator hopefully has a few sample pieces, or check out a website like *http://www.etsy.com*, or *http://www.pinterest.com* for some more inspiration.

Guys like jewelry too, so make sure there are options available that may appeal to them if they choose to participate in this program.

*"I grew up in libraries, and I hope I've learned never to take them for granted. A thriving library is the heart of its community, providing access to information and educational opportunities, bringing people together, leveling the playing field, and archiving our history." –*
*Josie Brown*

# #55 – Teens in the garden

I have talked a lot about instilling a sense of community ownership at the library. This program achieves this goal and adds beauty. If the library has grounds, consider seriously, adding this program to the list. Give the Teen Council, or a group of teens the freedom to design, plant and maintain a space of their own.

**Target Audience:** Teens

**Things needed:**
- A Facilitator
- A planting space
- Bulbs
- Bulb planters or small trowels/shovels
- Planting mix
- A weather-proof sign (optional)
- Other plants (optional)
- Snacks & drinks (optional)

**Prep Time:** Time to allow the teens to craft their plan, then purchase the requested items.

**Program Time:** 2 sessions (one planning, one planting). The actual work time will depend on the size of the group and the size of the project.

**Number of Participants:** A small group works best, but registration is not recommended. If more participants show up than expected, put them to work weeding and pruning.

**Number of Friends/Volunteers needed:** 1 to facilitate and help guide the work.

**How/Notes:** If the library is owned by the city, there may be a permission process before altering the grounds. On the upside, the city might pay for the planting materials.

Consider planting bulbs in the shape of something (the flag, stripes of the school colors, a rainbow)

Should there be a border? Should the planting area be angled (raised on one side) so it can be seen well? (This may interfere with sprinkler systems or run-off areas, so plan carefully)

*"Libraries are necessary gardens, unsurpassed at growing excitement"*
*– J. Patrick Lewis, Please Bury Me in the Library*

# #56 – Finals study session

Host a finals study session each night of finals week for the high school patrons and they will be very grateful. Make it even better by inviting the teachers of the classes. Throw out some snacks and create a space for preparation. Worried faces will enter and hopefully, confident faces will leave.

**Target Audience:** Teens

**Things needed:**
- Volunteer tutors
- A dedicated space (semi-private to private is preferred)
- The library's resources on the subject of concentration
- Snacks (optional)

**Prep Time:** Minimal to arrange space and set out snacks

**Program Time:** 2-3 hours

**Number of Participants:** Try to keep it to a dull roar – top end is the fire code

**Number of Friends/Volunteers needed:** 1 to set up and clean up

**How/Notes:** This program is drop-in and self-directed. That doesn't mean that there shouldn't be rules and monitoring. Make sure everyone is aware that the time needs to be dedicated to studying, and that's all. The name of the game here is RESPECT.

# #57 – Glow-in-the-dark scavenger hunt

The library after dark? Fun! This program can be done as a stand-alone, or as part of a movie night, sleepover at the Library (Program #42) or other nighttime event. Writing riddles to find the items would add to the fun and difficulty level of the scavenger hunt. To up the difficulty level even more, have different lists for different teams so that not all items are meant to be gathered by all teams. Points off for collecting the wrong item!

**Target Audience:** Tweens - Teens

**Things needed:**
- Glow-in-the-dark paint
- Small scavenger hunt items (enough so that each team can find what they need). Think about items like: pennies, silk flowers, rocks, paper clips, die-cast cars, or wooden letters (blocks) that will spell out the answer to the riddle (plus decoy letters).
- A checklist with pen or pencil
- A bag to hold items (if they are to be collected)
- A fun treasure hunting movie (*National Treasure, Sahara or Raiders of the Lost Ark*)(optional)
- Snacks (optional)

**Prep Time:** Some time is needed to collect the items, paint and hide them, and prepare the scavenger hunt checklists. Minimal time to set up movie and lay out snacks.

**Program Time:** 1-3 hours depending on whether a movie is shown or not.

**Number of Participants:** 15 would be optimum. Smaller libraries or venues may want to reduce the number to 10. But 5 teams is best.

**Number of Friends/Volunteers needed:** 1-2

**How/Notes:** Prizes would be fun, but not necessary. Some helpful websites are:

*http://www.riddleme.com*
*http://www.buzzle.com*
*http://www.coolest-kid-birthday-parties.com*

*"A good library will never be too neat, or too dusty, because somebody will always be in it, taking books off the shelves and staying up late reading them."* - Lemony Snicket, *Horseradish*

# #58 – Playing music – Introduction to different instruments

Schools across the country have had to sacrifice music programs as resources have dwindled. With that in mind and looking to fill the gap, I wanted the library to be able provide an alternative. But, when I first considered hosting an introduction to instruments program at the library, my brain could only think of wind instruments like oboes, trumpets, saxophones and bassoons. The thought of passing those around grossed me out, so I tabled the idea. Then, my brother gave my son a roll-up keyboard and the idea was reborn. Of course! There are tons of great instruments to play that aren't festering germ pools. Bring in drums, keyboards, hand bells, harps, guitars or sitars. Add some simple songs and make some music!

**Target Audience:** Tweens-Teens (and younger if the music is simple enough and the group small)

**Things needed:**
- A volunteer Facilitator/Instructor
- A variety of instruments (or get several of one kind and focus on one instrument per session)
- Sheets for finger placement (optional)
- Music featuring the instruments being introduced
- Simple songs
- Semi-private to private space

**Prep Time:** Minimal to arrange space

**Program Time:** An hour

**Number of Participants:** Recommend registration for this program and keep the numbers low so that everyone gets a chance to play.

**Number of Friends/Volunteers needed:** 1-2 (Facilitator/Instructor and one to make sure equal playing time is achieved)
**How/Notes:** Sanitation is still important; keep things clean.

If enough instruments are available, consider focusing on one instrument each session and advertise as a series.

Consider providing resources of local music instructors.

*Libraries are anything but quiet: they resound with centuries of knowledge and human experience -- and I can think of no more perfect music!" Kristen Kittscher*

# #59 – Minecraft (or other cool game) introduction/demonstration

Now that it has its own convention and has grown exponentially in the past few years, Minecraft has my attention, and the attention of millions of young gamers all over the world. Seize the opportunity and use the game's popularity to get new patrons into the library. Or, if something new comes along, embrace it and find a way to connect the library to the craze.

**Target Audience:** Young Gamers

**Things needed:**
- A Presenter/Facilitator
- The Minecraft demo on a few computers
- Some tips & tricks

**Prep Time:** Minimal to arrange space

**Program Time:** 1 ½ hours or enough for every participant to play

**Number of Participants:** Limited by space and fire code, but recommend participants be limited to the number of computers available, so registration should be considered.

**Number of Friends/Volunteers needed:** 1-2 skilled Minecraft players to serve as Presenters/Facilitators

**How/Notes:** If it is possible to link the games together and play in a forum, that will help facilitate understanding and the participant's enjoyment of the game. If not, consider a presentation of the basics of the game, then allow participants to play with guidance from the Presenter/Facilitator.

Make sure the Presenter/Facilitator offers plenty of tips and tricks, but not cheat codes.

# #60 – Cartooning

The basics of cartooning are really, well, basic. Cartooning is layering shapes and embellishing to produce a picture. It only looks hard. When participants are shown a few starter cartoons, they'll be off and running with creativity. This program could easily be done as a series (cartooning faces, animals, heroes & villains, backgrounds & places) or as a demo during a larger event like the Photography Photo Challenge and Art Show (Program #192)

**Target Audience:** Tweens & Teens – Anyone interested

**Things needed:**
- An Instructor
- Audiovisual support (projector, overhead, white board or large easel with butcher paper)
- Drawing pads or paper
- Pencils
- Erasers
- Colored pencils or markers for finishing (optional)
- Tables for participants to work (the Instructor will dictate space arrangement)
- The library's resources on the topic
- Snacks (optional)

**Prep Time:** Less than ½ hour to arrange space and lay out snacks (or save snacks to the end and have the volunteer handle it)

**Program Time:** An hour

**Number of Participants:** Recommend registration for this program and the Instructor decides how many participants is appropriate. Less than 15 recommended.

**Number of Friends/Volunteers needed:** 1 if serving snacks, otherwise the Instructor can handle the program.

**How/Notes:** Instructor will decide the format. But possibilities include:

- Giving out pre-made "How To" booklets and having participants work while Instructor provides guidance
- Instructor shows a technique and everyone goes and practices
- Students gather around the Instructor and work alongside, then free-flow for awhile
- Hang step-by-step samples around the room and participants choose to try the ones they like

No matter the format chosen, this is a fun program that will be well attended.

Make sure the library resources on drawing and cartooning are on display and available for checkout.

Be ready! If the Instructor can't make it, look online for help. Try: *http://www.authorstream.com/Presentation/acLiLtocLiMB-625767-how-to-draw-cartoon-characters-basic-instructions/*

# #61 – Book recommendations

My local book store was a wonderful place. Sadly, they closed, but one of the cool things they did was book recommendations. People wrote a short synopsis of the book and why they recommend it. A recommendation provides the browser that little extra push they need to say "yes!" to a book. Knowing someone else has read and endorses a book helps make the decision to give a book a chance. Blank index cards with a fold at the top work great for this project.

**Target Audience:** Teens

**Things needed:**
- Well-read teens
- Index cards
- Tape

**Prep Time:** None – just get the word out to the Teen Council or ask teen patrons

**Program Time:** Ongoing

**Number of Participants:** Limitless

**Number of Friends/Volunteers needed:** 1 to handle posting the cards and removing tattered or otherwise damaged cards.

**How/Notes:** This could be used by the middle and high school English/Reading teachers as an ongoing assignment or extra credit project.

Spread the cards out throughout the stacks. One author with seven recommendations cards is unnecessary and clutters up the shelves. Too many for a shelf or section? Keep extra reviews in reserve and rotate them often.

# #62 – Career interest activity & discussion

"What should I do with my life?" "I have so many interests, how do I choose?" Classic life questions asked by teenagers everywhere. This program aims to help those struggling teens by having them help themselves and each other through a collage-art project and discussion. This is quite an eye-opening experience for many teens.

**Target Audience:** Teens

**Things needed:**
- A Facilitator
- Magazines – many of them on a variety of topics
- Small poster boards (or 11x14 construction paper)
- Glue sticks
- Scissors (enough for everyone, or nearly everyone)
- Snacks (optional)

**Prep Time:** Time to gather magazines. Plus about 15 minutes to lay out supplies.

**Program Time:** 2 hours. 45 minutes to an hour to complete collages, then an hour for presentation and discussion.

**Number of Participants:** 10-15 is optimum

**Number of Friends/Volunteers needed:** 1 + Facilitator if providing snacks, otherwise, the Facilitator can handle the program.

**How/Notes:** Participants should be instructed to cut out pictures that "speak" to them, or just that they really like. Words and phrases are neither encouraged, nor discouraged, but pictures are best. Participants should cut out the pictures and create a collage on the provided paper.

Then, after the collages are complete, participants will take turns sharing their collages and why they like the pictures they've chosen.

The other participants will ask questions and offer career suggestions based on the collage presented. A presentation could go something like this:

PRESENTER (whose collage has a lot of snowboarding pictures on it): "I really like being outside in winter, snowboarding, so my collage is mostly pictures of snowboarding"

GROUP or FACILITATOR: "What is it you like most about snowboarding? Is it being outside in winter, or do you like challenging yourself to try new things? Do you like teaching people about snowboarding, or talking about what new moves people are doing?"

** Questions that aren't directly related to snowboarding will help the Presenter see that there may be career opportunities in the realm of snowboarding, without actually being a professional snowboarder. S/he could write for a winter sports magazine, be an instructor, design boards or product test equipment. The important part of this program is to serve as a guide to show participants that there are many opportunities to pursue which will allow them to continue to be involved in the things that make them happy now.

As another benefit of the program, participants who may have had little direction before, will begin to have a clearer picture of themselves. Presenters will show, through their words and non-verbal cues, which photos mean more to them than others and the audience will pick up those cues. An audience member may say "You know, when you talk about healthy foods, your face just lights up, and your enthusiasm is obvious". PRESENTER: "Wow, I never knew that good nutrition meant so much to me. Maybe I should consider being a dietician or chef!"

# #63 – Henna body art

A symbol of celebration in India, a henna body art program will potentially be expensive with few participants. But, timing is everything with this program. Do it about a week before Prom or Homecoming and the library will be talked about nearly as much as the dresses and decorations.

**Target Audience:** Teens

**Things needed:**
- An Artist/Instructor (it is possible to find someone willing to lend their time for the practice if the Friends purchase the supplies)
- Henna supplies (which will be included if a professional is hired)
- Music (optional but recommended)
- Snacks (optional)

**Prep Time:** ½ hour to arrange space, set out snacks and set up music

**Program Time:** 2 hours

**Number of Participants:** Will be dictated by the Instructor and supplies available. Registration will be required.

**Number of Friends/Volunteers needed:** 1 + Artist/Instructor

**How/Notes:** The best resource I've found about henna is *http://www.hennapage.com*

You could purchase the supplies and do this program as a workshop, but hiring a professional will net a much more enjoyable experience.

A permission slip is an absolute must for this program. If the library already has a standard release form, use that. Otherwise look at the American Library Association website for a sample.

# #64 – Cupcake decorating "war"

This program could stand-alone, but would also be fun as part of the 100 best of all time movies (Program #102) or sleepover at the library (Program #42). Participants will decorate their cupcakes, then vote for their favorites. Small prizes or bragging rights to the victor & cupcakes for everyone!

**Target Audience:** Teens – Anyone interested

**Things needed:**
- Plain cupcakes – Remember to post allergen information
- A variety of colored frostings
- A variety of decorating materials (tips, bags, sprinkles, gum paste)
- Music (optional)
- Pen & paper (voting slips and for sketching cupcake designs)
- Container for votes
- Small prizes (optional)

**Prep Time:** Time to make or buy plain cupcakes and materials. ½ hour to lay everything out.

**Program Time:** An hour

**Number of Participants:** Recommend registration to ensure sufficient number of cupcakes and supplies

**Number of Friends/Volunteers needed:** 1

**How/Notes:** This program would be great as a Teen Council project. It would also be good as a "get to know you" event for a newly elected Teen Council.
- Decide on a theme
- Set a 20-30 minute time limit for design and decorating
- Put on some music on to get the creative juices flowing

- Give each participant 2 cupcakes (one for practice)
- Consider a theme (Spring, the Color Purple, Jungle, Zombie Apocalypse)
- Set out the cupcakes and assign each one a number
- Give each participant a voting slip – collect the votes and announce the winners
- EAT!

*"My best friend is a person who will give me a book I have not read." Abraham Lincoln*

# #65 - Sandwich making party

A sandwich making party can be part of another event, or stand alone on its own. The best part about a sandwich making party is how easy it is. And, just like black, it goes with everything. Try pairing it with story time, a nutrition discussion, teen council, the library's birthday party celebration (Program #180) or a Meatless Monday (Program #146) demo. In all cases this program will add a memorable element to the event that will have patrons interested in what's coming up next. "Feed them, and they will come."

**Target Audience:** Teens to Everyone

**Things needed:**
- Sandwich making "stuff" – a variety of breads or wraps, peanut butter, jelly, cheeses, cold cuts, veggies, condiments, or other program appropriate fillings. Use tapenades, hummus & artisan breads for a "Meatless Monday" (Program #146) idea party. Yummy!
- Knives
- Plates
- Napkins
- Something to drink w/cups
- Tablecloth

**Prep Time:** Not long, maybe 15 – 30 minutes for set-up + shopping.

**Program Time:** However long it takes for participants to make and enjoy their sandwiches.

**Number of Participants:** Varies depending on the event tie-in or space available.

**Number of Friends/Volunteers needed:** 1-2

**How/Notes:**

- Shop for the decided upon menu items. It is possible to get the items donated, so don't forget to ask
- Set up tables
- Enjoy!

Be cautious of food allergies, especially nuts. It is advised to segregate the peanut butter from the other sandwich fixings.

Consider putting the bread in the middle; sometimes that is enough. Notify participants of the allergens present prior to entrance into the food area.

Try doing a taste test and voting on favorites.

# #66 - Typing class

Children are introduced to computers at a very early age. When they are little, they usually only use the mouse or up and down arrows on the keyboard. But, by second-third grade they are beginning to use the computer for school reports. By fifth grade, they'll likely be regularly using the keyboard to produce work. Now is the time to offer a typing class (or younger if there is interest or need). Learning proper technique will help immeasurably. Actual keyboarding classes are sometimes the victim of school budget cuts, so it would be nice to offer an alternative. Class could run for several weeks, duplicated once a quarter or every 6 months, depending on interest and demand.

**Target Audience:** 9-15 year olds – anyone interested

**Things needed:**
- An Instructor
- Keyboard covers (no peeking!)
- Practice sheets
- Computers or typewriters
- Paper stands (optional)

**Prep Time:** Minimal if the machines are already set up.

**Program Time:** An hour

**Number of Participants:** Depends on available machines. Registration will be required for this program.

**Number of Friends/Volunteers needed:** The Instructor and one volunteer should be able to handle this program with ease.

**How/Notes:** Recruit an Instructor and ask for a lesson plan. Make sure they know the program run time and the number of registrants.

# #67 – Gaming system tournaments

Some libraries are lucky enough to have a dedicated space for a gaming system. Others purchase a gaming system for patron use and bring it out on special occasions, like a... tournament.

**Target Audience:** Tweens & Teens

**Things needed:**
- Facilitator
- Game System
- Games that lend themselves well to a tournament (think short games like Wii bowling, Xbox Kinnect games, Rock Band, dancing games, Mario cart etc.)
- Comfortable seating for those playing and watching
- Tournament bracket sheet
- Small prizes for winners (optional)
- Snacks (optional, but highly recommended)

**Prep Time:** Less than an hour to prep space and put out snacks

**Program Time:** Will depend on number of participants. Adjust the number of participants to the game chosen so the program time stays under 2 hours.

**Number of Participants:** Will depend on space and games chosen, registration may be needed.

**Number of Friends/Volunteers needed:** 1-2 including Facilitator

**How/Notes:** There are those with the opinion that gaming systems have no place in a library. I disagree with, but respect this opinion and always encourage Friends groups to choose programming that is appropriate for their mission and patrons.

# #68 – Poetry

Poetry is widely misunderstood, but lovingly embraced by some. Poetry "slams," writer's workshops, contests, readings, or pairing poetry with a song-writing workshop (Program #132); any of these would make a great series. Challenge regular participants to bring a friend to reach a new audience of future poetry enthusiasts.

**Target Audience:** Teens - Adults

**Things needed:** This will vary depending on the program chosen, however, basically:
- A Facilitator/Instructor
- Pens, pencils, colored pencils, paper
- The library's resources on the type of poetry being discussed
- Examples of the topic poems
- For readings: Stools or podium; microphone (optional)

**Prep Time:** No program will take longer than 15 minutes to set-up

**Program Time:** All programs except the contest should take about an hour

**Number of Participants:** Poetry groups are best kept fairly small (no more than 10), so registration is recommended.

**Number of Friends/Volunteers needed:** 1

**How/Notes:** Dedicate time to various poetry forms (Acrostic, Haiku, Sensory, Free verse, Limericks, Couplets)

Start with a read-aloud to inspire the poets assembled.

Consider putting first line options into a hat. Someone pulls the line and everyone writes off of the chosen first line. Or, how about who can use the fewest words to convey a complex thought or idea?

Discuss famous poets and their works wither through analysis or appreciation.

Be prepared for this program to morph into some sort of writing group. Hey! Next program...

*"Only in a library can you travel the world, become anyone, and experience anything while sitting still! As both an author and active member of my local Friends of the Library group, I see firsthand how much our library means to our community. It's not only a place to perform research, it's a link to services, an entertainment venue, and a cultural center." Diane Kelly*

# #69 – Writing/critique groups

Writers who love to write, will write no matter what; they just can't help it. They must. put. words. on. paper. But, even the most dedicated writer won't thrive without support. Teens don't usually fit neatly into adult writing groups, which are typically separated into genres. Without support, it is more probable than just possible, that the interest of enthusiastic teen writers will wane and the world may be deprived of a really talented writer. Don't let that happen! Start a Teen Writing Group today and give aspiring writers space and time to share their work with each other.

**Target Audience:** Teens

**Things needed:**
- A Facilitator
- A set of guidelines (this needs to be a working critique group and everyone needs to understand how to give feedback without being hurtful or discouraging)
- A format – will participants submit work to each other via email before the group meets? Will they share work during the meeting and get feedback there? Will one person facilitate (recommended), and will that job rotate? (also recommended)
- Snacks (optional)

**Prep Time:** Minimal to arrange space

**Program Time:** 1-2 hours – let the group decide

**Number of Participants:** If the group gets larger than 8-10, consider breaking into genres

**Number of Friends/Volunteers needed:** 1 if providing snacks. This could be the job of the Facilitator. They'll need to be aware of their clean-up responsibilities.

**How/Notes:** Program frequency will depend on the teens and the size of the group. They may naturally morph into genres or possibly a gender split.

Some folks have an aversion to sharing their work with a group for fear of having it taken or plagiarized somehow. Address this in the guidelines.

Periodically review the standing guidelines and adjust as needed.

*"Libraries made me a writer, but more importantly, they made me a thinker." Sarah Darer Littman*

# #70 – Survival bracelets

Military grade parachute cord, or paracord, is now available in nearly any color imaginable. Making paracord into usable survival bracelets is a fun craft enjoyed by tweens and teens, boys and girls alike. Talk about ways to use the paracord in an emergency situation and provide a small knot tying guide (a few samples printed on a sheet would suffice). The result is a well-rounded, fun program with wearable advertisement for what the library has to offer.

**Target Audience:** Tweens & Teens

**Things needed:**
- An Instructor/Facilitator
- Paracord in a few colors (maybe the local middle or high school's spirit colors?)
- ½" – ⅝" plastic clasp clips
- Something to hold the project in place while working on it. Strong clip with magnetic board, or duct tape are options.
- Knot tying take home sheet (optional)
- Paracord survival uses take home sheet (optional)
- Snacks (optional)

**Prep Time:** About ½ hour to set up space

**Program Time:** An hour

**Number of Participants:** 15 is ideal for this program. Any more would limit the Instructor/Facilitator's ability to provide individual attention when needed. Registration recommended.

**Number of Friends/Volunteers needed:** 1 + Instructor/Facilitator
**How/Notes:** Try: _Paracord 101: A Beginner's Guide to Paracord Bracelets and Projects_ by Todd Mikkelsen
Or, consider a kit: Make Your Own Paracord Wristbands by Creativity for Kids is a kit that claims to have enough supplies to make 8 wristbands.

# #71 – Duct tape

No longer just for heating and air conditioning work, holes in screen doors or dangling mufflers. No! Duct tape has become an art medium enjoyed by millions. Duct tape comes in so many varieties, it seems as if you can't even count them all. I even purchased glow-in-the-dark duct tape for my Dad for his birthday and my niece received a tower of duct tape for Christmas with plaid, rainbow and cupcakes prints! I'm even hearing of duct tape themed birthday parties where kids craft the day away making everything from heart-shaped purses to clothes for their dolls and wallets for their parents. I love it when creativity meets function.

**Target Audience:** Tweens - Teens

**Things needed:**
- An Instructor/Facilitator
- Duct tape
- Some sample project sheets
- Extra supplies and embellishments (will depend on projects selected)
- Scissors
- Workspace
- Music (optional)

**Prep Time:** Minimal to arrange space and set out supplies

**Program Time:** An hour

**Number of Participants:** Registration recommended and limit to 10-15 participants

**Number of Friends/Volunteers needed:** 1 + Instructor/Facilitator

**How/Notes:** Cover the following during instruction:
- How to make "fabric"
- Edging

- Flowers
- Fixing mistakes

Consider a few basic projects. Survey participants or offer a "menu" of a few options (for example: wallet, coin purse, flower pen, key chain, or bangle bracelet to name a few) that participants can choose when they register.

*When I discovered libraries, it was like having Christmas every day." Jean Fritz*

# #72 – Craft – Bling up the box

Couple a plain box with sparkly jewels, glitter glue, stickers and enthusiastic crafters and what do you get? A creatively tricked out, blinged out jewelry/stuff box, that's what. This program is best as a stand-alone make and take, or coupled with a movie (preferably something with a treasure box – perhaps *Treasure Planet* or *National Treasure*).

**Target Audience:** 9-14 year olds

**Things needed:**
- Facilitator(s)
- A few samples
- Unfinished boxes. (photo boxes, wooden boxes, or paper maché boxes)
- Jewels and sequins – get a variety pack
- Glitter glue pens
- Regular glue or glue gun (CAUTION! Grown-ups or low heat please)
- Stickers
- Gel pens/markers
- Paint w/paint supplies (optional but recommended. Will need to factor in drying time)
- Music (optional)

**Prep Time:** About ½ hour to set up space and lay out supplies

**Program Time:** 1-3 hours depending on whether or not a movie is included

**Number of Participants:** This is a self-directed project, the number will be limited only by space and budget for supplies. Recommend registration on this program and registration should be capped at 10% less than supplies purchased.

**Number of Friends/Volunteers needed:** Facilitators: 1 for up to 15 participants, 2 for more than 15.

**How/Notes:** Lay out the supplies, issue the box at registration/check-in and watch the creativity flow. If drying time is needed, consider making slips of paper for participants to write their name on and slide under their project. That way participants will be able to remember which one is theirs when it is time to go home.

Arrange another short activity for drying time; perhaps a brainstorming session for other programs that would appeal to the participants present. Write the ideas on butcher block on invite one of the participants to scribe.

Another possible activity – Reader's Theatre (Program #73).

# #73 – Reader's theatre

Reader's theatre is a marvelous way for budding actors to try their hand at acting, but also as a literacy activity to enhance understanding of a story. For traditional reader's theatre, there are no props, stage sets, or costumes. Actors openly display their scripts and read their lines. So this program can be done anywhere, any time!

**Target Audience:** Tweens (but the script chosen will dictate the target age range – think about doing different ones to reach everyone)

**Things needed:**
- An Instructor/Facilitator
- A fun script – with copies for everyone
- Refreshments (optional)

**Prep Time:** Prep time will be focused on choosing a script, making copies and arranging space. About an hour total

**Program Time:** An hour

**Number of Participants:** Will depend on the script chosen and whether or not an audience is desired.

**Number of Friends/Volunteers needed:** 1-2

**How/Notes:** There are several websites with free, and for purchase scripts for reader's theatre. Also, a reader's theatre script could be a project of the creative writing workshop (Program #38), used in the conversational language series (Program #104) or as an activity during the Sleepover at the Library (Program #42).
Website resources:
*http://www.aaronshep.com*
*http://www.readerstheaterallyear.com*

# #74 – Spa day – Make lotions & potions

This program is made for tweens and teens, many of whom, like my daughter and her friends, love the idea of putting on a "spa" at home. What participants will do in this program, is learn a little bit about lotions and aromatherapy, then make homemade lotion using a lotion base and essential oils they choose themselves. They will also fill and sew a soothing face mask they can microwave and use to ease away the troubles of a hard day at school, or give as a gift to someone special.

**Target Audience:** Tweens-Teens

**Things needed:**
- An Instructor/Facilitator – consider contacting a whole foods store, or massage therapist to facilitate with advice on essential oils and their therapeutic uses.
- A lotion base
- Some essential oils – if a massage therapist, or someone who regularly uses oils comes in, it might be possible to use their oils and be charged either a flat fee or somehow keep track of what's used and pay that way.
- Eye-droppers (for transferring oils from their containers to the lotion base)
- Mixing bowls + wooden sticks
- Small bottles or decorative containers for the lotion
- Labels
- Markers and/or colored pencils
- Pre-made cotton fabric pouches sewn with a 1" opening. (Pouches should have a finished size of 6"x3" and make sure to have a few extra available just in case)
- Dry rice or lentils to fill the pouches
- Either dry lavender or other recommended dry herbs or essential oils
- Needle & thread (to match the pouches)
- Soothing music (optional but recommended)

**Prep Time:** Time to make the pouches and get supplies together, and less than ½ hour to lay it all out.

**Program Time:** 1 – 1 ½ hours

**Number of Participants:** Recommend no more than 15 participants

**Number of Friends/Volunteers needed:** 1 + Instructor/facilitator

**How/Notes:** This program should begin with a discussion about the therapeutic benefits of aromatherapy and relaxation, along with which scents stimulate which types of responses.

Each participant should leave with a finished lotion and therapy pouch. Other options include lip balm, lip gloss or body glitter.

The pouches, when microwaved for a minute (no more!) can be used as a soothing heating pad to lay across tired eyes, or a sore knee etc.

# #75 – Magic workshop

Abracadabra, Alacazam! Pick a card, any card. After participation in this program, participants will be able to delight and amaze!

**Target Audience:** Ages 8-13

**Things needed:**
- An Instructor
- Supplies for a few simple magic tricks (will depend on the tricks chosen)
- Instruction sheets for participants to take home

**Prep Time:** Minimal to arrange space

**Program Time:** An hour

**Number of Participants:** Registration is recommended and will be limited to Instructor preference and amount of supplies.

**Number of Friends/Volunteers needed:** 1 + Instructor

**How/Notes:** Consider a discussion about different elements or genres of magic (close-up magic, illusions, math tricks, mind-reading and prediction tricks, card tricks). Also talk about famous magicians and their contributions to magic. I found these few simple magic tricks, among others on *http://www.about.com* and all could be considered appropriate for the target audience.
- Killer card prediction
- Magic coin dish
- The deciding domino
- The color spelling trick
- The vanishing bead

Remind participants that there are a few cardinal rules about magic. Wayne Kawamoto in an about.com article describes them as follows:
1. Thou shalt Never tell the Secret!

2. Thou shalt practice, practice, and practice!
3. Thou shalt entertain – the audience wants a show (which is much more than the show itself)
4. Thou shalt respect thy audiences (don't be smug because you know the trick and they don't)

*"Libraries are about books. Books have no color. And they don't care who reads them." - Augusta Scattergood,* <u>Glory Be</u>

*The door available to everyone that can lead to happiness and success is the modest door of the public library. I found it to be so in my own life and work." Herman Wouk*

*" Here was one place where I could find out who I was and what I was going to become. And that was the public library."* - Jerzy Kosinski

# Chapter 4 – Seniors to adults of all ages

When it comes to the over 55 crowd, prevailing wisdom across most businesses is that if you haven't captured their attention by now, you aren't going to. They are either in, or they are out. They've found their path and they are traveling it on their own. Wrong! The fact is that you really can reach this audience, but the motivator has to be really, really good. The lucky seniors who are also retirees, theoretically have more discretionary time than everyone else. But today, seniors are FAR more active in supporting their communities than in generations past and are more giving of their time in unique and creative ways. They succinctly understand the value of their time, so programming for this group has got to be "spot on" to capture their attention and hopefully gain some of that available volunteer time. If done well, thoughtful programming will give seniors a new enthusiasm for this long lost treasure – the library. Make sure that programs are a good mix of must-have information and soul-food, meaning programs designed to inspire and excite the imagination. Do this and they will show up for almost everything you offer. This is also the group most likely to share their opinions about the programs offered. Ask often, listen closely, and respond!

A few notes about websites (or the senior programming page on the library's website) and development of on-screen materials for seniors. The natural aging of the eye effects screen vision. So consider the following:

- Avoid use of narrow or condensed fonts
- Use clear fonts, avoid novelty typefaces
- When inserting hyperlinks, make sure the links have a different color
- Double space text
- Break up large pieces of text into smaller segments designed to be read on-screen
- Avoid patterned backgrounds
- Avoid excessive animation

- Use active voice
- Utilize a clean, straightforward organization of website with clear groupings

*"In a good bookroom you feel in some mysterious way that you are absorbing the wisdom contained in all the books through your skin, without even opening them." - Mark Twain*

# #76 – Healthy, wealthy, nifty & thrifty series

What brings health & wealth? Being nifty and thrifty, of course! Seriously though, this program is intended as an uplifting look into living better. Trying new things, trimming the fat (literally and figuratively) will create an outlook for living the "Golden Years" with a rejuvenated enthusiasm.

**Target Audience:** Seniors

**Things needed:**
- Dynamic, interesting Speakers/Presenters
- Audiovisual support
- Refreshments (optional but encouraged)

**Prep Time:** Minimal to ½ hour, depending on presentation

**Program Time:** 1 – 1 ½ hours depending on presentation

**Number of Participants:** Limited only by space and fire code

**Number of Friends/Volunteers needed:** 1 + Speaker/Presenter

**How/Notes:** Recommend this program be in the evening to offset any standing coffee chat (Program #87), since the two programs are somewhat similar in design. While the coffee chat is meant to be an opportunity to regularly get together with periodic presentations or events, this series is more educational in its approach.
- Diets aimed at healthy living (raw foods, vegetarian, paleo) (healthy)
- Decoding food labels (healthy)
- New health slants (belly dancing, holistic gardening, aromatherapy) (healthy)
- Sharing knowledge through tutoring (healthy/wealthy)
- Investment opportunities vs. scams (wealthy)
- Crafting for income (wealthy)

- How to start a consulting service (wealthy)
- Graphic design (wealthy/nifty)
- Fashion (nifty)
- Card clutches (bridge, hearts, cribbage, euchre, pinochle)(nifty)
- Auto restoration (nifty)
- Antiques (nifty)
- Digitizing photo memories (nifty)
- Arts (photography, painting, scale models) (nifty)
- Tinker Talents Night. How about a night where skilled repairers tackle small repair jobs for people? Shoes, clothes, small appliances, electronics all could be addressed (nifty/thrifty and nice)
- Making homemade products (thrifty)
- Finding local deals (apps and websites dedicated to saving money)(thrifty)
- Bartering (thrifty)

Lots of things could fall into a series like this. Think about what might drive interest – the sky's the limit. Oh, hey! There's another one – Remote controlled helicopter workshop. Now that's nifty!

# #77 – Computer classes

In a conversation with my mom, we were talking about the health benefits for the brain when engaging in the taxing activity of trying to learn a new language. I asked what language she was considering, and she said "I'm going to try to learn the language of my new iPad mini. I think that will be only slightly easier than learning Russian." Spot on mama! Of course she was kidding, but she is right where many people are – computer language is a foreign language. A great, safe, place to jump in, is at the library.

**Target Audience:** Seniors or anyone interested in learning computer basics

**Things needed:**
- An Instructor/Facilitator (a patient one)
- A lesson plan
- Computers

**Prep Time:** Minimal to arrange space

**Program Time:** An hour

**Number of Participants:** Limit to the number of computers available. Registration is recommended.

**Number of Friends/Volunteers needed:** 1 (The Instructor/Facilitator can handle this program)

**How/Notes:** This program can range from formal step-by-step instruction to self-paced, follow-a-guide, to an open forum where folks can just simply get their questions asked.

# #78 – How to use the Internet

"Get on board, or get left behind." Many seniors who have resisted learning about the world-wide web are feeling the pinch of not having the access they need. Whether it be online medical appointment scheduling, or form processing, or wanting to order flowers for a far-away friend; the Internet can be quite handy. When we first introduced this program at my home library, the Managing Librarian conducted the program to an enthusiastic audience. She discussed basic navigation and answered the biggest question and the main reason for resistance – "What IS the Internet?" And, its follow on question – "How does it work?" It is much easier to get on board with something when there is a basic understanding of what it is and how it works. Follow-on classes could address Internet security, payment systems, utilizing search engines, the differences between http & https, .com, .org, .gov & .net, where to access government resources like Social Security Administration (SSA), IRS, and Medicare.

**Target Audience:** Seniors

**Things needed:**
- An Instructor/Facilitator
- A computer for each participant or pair of participants
- A tablet and pen or pencil for each participant for taking notes (optional)
- Refreshments (optional)

**Prep Time:** The Instructor/Facilitator should prepare talking points, otherwise, prep time is only needed to set out refreshments if they are being offered.

**Program Time:** An hour

**Number of Participants:** Depends on the number of available computers. Recommend registration.

**Number of Friends/Volunteers needed:** 1

**How/Notes:** It might be handy to prepare a navigation "how to" with screen snapshots for each session.

This program works well as a series (Internet 101, 201 etc.)

Consider compiling the classes into a User Guide available at the desk where people sign up to use the computers, so the class can be self-directed.

# #79 – End-of-life issues series

This topic is not fun to talk about. But for some, the luck of life has been on their side and they have reached a point in life where it has become necessary to give consideration to a good quality of life as they approach the inevitable end. And thoughts also turn to ensuring that the legacy of their hard work is protected for their family into the future. Good planning will be appreciated by those left behind. While talking about these issues may be difficult, the alternative is to ignore them, which may lead to confusion and arguments amongst children, spouses and courts. Nobody wants to strap their families with unnecessary burden. This program will help address how to handle some of these tough topics.

**Target Audience:** Seniors

**Things needed:**
- A Presenter/Facilitator for each topic presented (could be the same person throughout the series, or a compilation of local expertise)
- Good resources
- Audiovisual support (if needed)
- Workbook (optional)
- Refreshments (optional)

**Prep Time:** About ½ hour to arrange space and set up audiovisual support

**Program Time:** 1 hour each

**Number of Participants:** Limited only by space and fire code

**Number of Friends/Volunteers needed:** 1 if serving refreshments, otherwise the Presenter/Facilitator can handle things.

**How/Notes:** Topics to consider:
- Long term care options

- Assisted living
- Living wills
- Trusts and annuities
- Wills – gifting and other estate plans (the who gets what issues)
- Burial plans
- Organ donation
- Hospice
- Is there a regular coffee chat (Program #87) at the library? These topics could be added. Or, consider these are part of the Healthy, wealthy, nifty and thrifty series (Program #76)

# #80 – Travelogues

Many parodies have been produced and performed about the pain of sitting through a slide show of someone's vacation. Shot after shot of unnamed landscapes or your aunt and uncle wearing hideous touristy clothes, standing, grinning in front of another unnamed museum or okay-that's-pretty-cool monument. For this program though, the travelogue should be a combination of dazzling photographs, coupled with real-life experiences, recommendations, words of caution (like rip-off cab companies, suspect water purity), money exchanges, safeguarding valuables, cuisine recommendations; anything that will inspire the travel bug within.

**Target Audience:** Seniors to anyone interested

**Things needed:**
- A Presenter – I think this would be a far less successful series if the Presenter remains the same for each "episode." Seek well-traveled volunteers, then build the series around the Presenters.
- Audiovisual support
- Refreshments (optional)

**Prep Time:** Minimal to arrange space

**Program Time:** 1 to 1 ½ hours

**Number of Participants:** Limited only by space and fire code

**Number of Friends/Volunteers needed:** 1

**How/Notes:** Keep the topic general enough to garner interest, but not too broad. "Fine foods of Europe" or, "Outdoor adventures in the Caribbean" may be more interesting than "South America."

# #81 – Health & Long-term care insurance

Navigating the health and long term care options available for seniors is a mind-numbing experience, on par with the volume of research required for a car or home purchase. These are all big decisions that should not be taken lightly. This program will help boil down the vast amount of information available into understandable English, so that participants can make more informed decisions.

**Target Audience:** Seniors

**Things needed:**
- An informed and impartial (this part is crucial!) Presenter. Look for a recently retired insurance agent, or local benefits counselor.
- Audiovisual support
- Comparison sheets
- Refreshments (optional)

**Prep Time:** Minimal to arrange space

**Program Time:** 1 hour on the half and half format. ½ hour for presentation, ½ hour for questions.

**Number of Participants:** Limited only by space and fire code

**Number of Friends/Volunteers needed:** 1 + Presenter

**How/Notes:** Make sure the Presenter is available for longer than an hour. These types of presentations often run over. It is likely that questions will outlast the time allotted.

Since a program like this, if advertised well, will bring non-regular library patrons into the library; consider an exit survey with questions about other senior topics that may be of interest in the community.

# #82 – Art series

Art is one of the things in life that has a tendency to get pushed to the back burner while we tackle the beast commonly referred to as "life," where it remains a dream to be pursued later. A dedicated few have produced art as their living, causing the rest of us to say "I wish I could do that." Well, it is never too late to embrace the inner artist. I recently met a man at my local art gallery and was awed by his work. I was absolutely floored when he told me that he drove truck for a living and didn't realize he had any art talent at all until he retired. What? His work was amazing and we had a nice talk about the benefits of trying something new. Bring a variety of art opportunities into the library and who knows? The next Grandma Moses (who didn't start painting until she was 76) may just walk in.

**Target Audience:** Seniors to anyone interested

**Things needed:**
- An Instructor/Facilitator
- Audiovisual support (if needed)
- A well ventilated space, depending on the medium being used
- Adequate space to work
- Supplies for the selected medium presented
- The library's resources on the topic discussed

**Prep Time:** About an hour to gather supplies and arrange space

**Program Time:** 1 – 1 ½ hours

**Number of Participants:** Registration is recommended as participants will need room to spread out. The number that can be accommodated will depend on the space available and the Instructor/Facilitator's preference.

**Number of Friends/Volunteers needed:** 1
**How/Notes:** Consider offering:

- Painting (watercolor, oil, acrylic)
- Oil pastels
- Pen & Ink
- Techniques (shadowing etc.)
- Silkscreen (though this gets quite messy)
- Pencil
- Photography
- Sculpture
- Weaving

*"I fall in love with any girl who smells of library paste."* - *Charles M. Schulz*

# #83 – The Historical Society

The main mission of any historical society is to preserve the history of the area, and show its relevance in today's society. This mission is typically achieved through outreach programs to schools and other civic groups and through partnerships with places like – the library.

**Target Audience:** Seniors – Anyone interested

**Things needed:**
- A Presenter/Facilitator who will present one of the Historical Society's outreach educational programs
- Audiovisual support if needed
- Refreshments (optional)

**Prep Time:** Minimal to arrange space

**Program Time:** An hour

**Number of Participants:** Limited only by space and fire code

**Number of Friends/Volunteers needed:** 1

**How/Notes:** Consider in partnership with the historical society, a project or outreach development that participants can help develop. Or, ask participants to bring old photos or memorabilia they'd be willing to donate to the historical society.

# #84 – Antique assessment

If the *Antiques Roadshow* television show isn't coming to town any time soon, you can still have some fun assessing patron treasures. It doesn't take an expert, just the Internet, and the library's resources along with someone who can navigate quickly to facilitate.

**Target Audience:** Seniors to anyone interested

**Things needed:**
- A Facilitator
- Computer access
- Some price books from the library's collection
- Patrons with antiques (discourage large items)
- A television with episodes of *Antiques Roadshow* or other program dedicated to assessment of antiques running in the background (optional)
- Refreshments for those waiting

**Prep Time:** ½ - 1 hour to arrange space. It might be fun to connect the computer to a projector so people who are waiting can see what's being evaluated.

**Program Time:** 1 ½ - 2 hours, however, if people are still waiting plan on going longer. If the program is really well attended, consider adding another date.

**Number of Participants:** Limited only limited by space and fire code.

**Number of Friends/Volunteers needed:** 1-2 savvy computer workers. One on computer, one on books, or just lay the books out so people can work together or on their own.

**How/Notes:** Provide a disclaimer releasing the library from liability if something is damaged.

# #85 – Wine and cheese tasting

Peanut butter and jelly, peas and carrots, Bert & Ernie; some things just go together. A robust glass of wine and a delicious slice of beautifully crafted cheese is no exception. If you are lucky enough to live in a wine or cheese producing area, consider focusing on local offerings. In any case, a wine and cheese tasting party is educational and fun. Have one for the next annual Friends of the Library meeting and it will probably increase attendance. Or, go bigger and use this program as a library fundraiser.

**Target Audience:** Adults

**Things needed:**
- A Facilitator – or consider inviting a sommelier to discuss the wine making process.
- Wine glasses (at least one per person, per wine with 15% overage available)
- Labels
- Serving area
- Cheese boards with knives
- Palate cleansers (fresh fruits, fresh vegetables, meats, crackers)
- 4 to 6 wines
- 3 to 5 cheeses
- Napkins
- The library's resources on the topic

**Prep Time:** Thought and consideration into which wines and cheeses to offer and shopping prior to the program. For the program, about ½ hour to an 1 hour to set-up depending on the number of registrants.

**Program Time:** Plan on 2 hours

**Number of Participants:** Less than 20 is preferred to keep costs down, but individual spaces may support a different number.

Recommend requiring registration so that the appropriate amount of resources are purchased.

**Number of Friends/Volunteers needed:** At least 2 to support the program or one per wine as pourers + a roamer to monitor trash

**How/Notes:** In general, pair like with like. For example, the full-bodied red wines are typically paired with stronger cheeses, while the lighter white wines go with the softer, milder cheeses.

Samples:
- Goat cheese or Camembert with Sauvignon Blanc or Cabernet
- Gorgonzola with Bordeaux or Port
- Sharp Cheddar with Shiraz
- Gouda or Chevre with Reisling

Make sure the temperatures are at their best: Cheese at room temperature, red wines at, or below room temperature, and white wines slightly chilled.

Consider purchasing a book on the topic as a gift for the library's collection.

How about getting a little goofy and doing a blind taste test using numbered brown paper bags?

Fun tidbit - January 20th is National Cheese Lover's Day

# #86 - Murder mystery at the library

Nancy Drew? Hardy Boys? Agatha Christie? Scooby Doo and the Gang? No. The super sleuths at the library for this entertaining program are the patrons! Murder mystery parties are great fun.

**Target Audience:** Adults

**Things needed:**
- An enthusiastic Facilitator
- A great story
- Refreshments

**Prep Time:** ½ hour or so to set up the space and refreshments

**Program Time:** Depends on which format or story is chosen, this program can be accomplished in 1-3 hours.

**Number of Participants:** Limit this to a dozen or less to keep things interesting – again, it will depend on the format chosen, some stories allow for more participants or an audience. Registration required.

**Number of Friends/Volunteers needed:** At least 2 including the Facilitator

**How/Notes:** Choose the game. *Note – when choosing a game, check the rating of the game. Some are inappropriate for a group expecting good, clean, fun. Gather the guests/suspects, and have a great time!

Make sure to note the suggested attire on advertising.

Try these websites for packages of scripts:
*http://www.nightofmystery.com/*
*http://www.mymysteryparty.com/adult.html*

# #87 – Coffee chat

The need, whether acknowledged or not, for human interaction, is ingrained in all of us. This simple program can become so many other things for the senior community. Allow it to morph over time; invite speakers sometimes, write sometimes, work sometimes (book repair perhaps?). Or sometimes, just set out the coffee and.... chat.

**Target Audience:** Adults

**Things needed:**
- Coffee, cups, napkins and coffee condiments
- A comfortable area in the library conducive to a group conversation

**Prep Time:** About ½ hour to brew coffee and set up coffee station

**Program Time:** An hour

**Number of Participants:** Limited only by space and fire code

**Number of Friends/Volunteers needed:** 1

**How/Notes:** Many of the other programs in this book lend themselves well to a coffee chat. Consider programs that are interactive with presentation and question/answer periods. For example, Genealogy tips & tricks (Program #92), or the End of life issues series (Program #79), or how about Life lists (Program #117)? What about pairing the coffee chat with the Home school connection (Program #162) or a pre-school story time? This is an opportunity to leverage knowledge and volunteerism. And, the list goes on...

Also consider:
- Inviting the mayor in from time to time
- Having the congressional representative stop by
- Writing get well cards for patrons

- Sending well wishes to overseas service members
- Tending the book sale
- Making audio recordings of duplicate books in the collection
- Planning and hosting a surprise birthday party for the managing librarian
- Taking the party on the road afterwards
    - Go to the Food Pantry to help out
    - Take materials to homebound patrons
    - Help the community theatre with set design and construction, or costume repair

# #88 – Social networking

Twitter & Facebook & Instagram – Oh my! Entering the world of social networking on the information super highway can be as scary as Dorothy and her companions facing their fears on the road to Oz. Social networking is a way for people to stay connected without actually regularly seeing each other face to face. And, there are definitely good and bad features with these sites. Navigation, security settings, common slang and protocol should be included in this program.

**Target Audience:** Seniors

**Things needed:**
- An Instructor/Facilitator – Ask for a volunteer (maybe someone who is a regular patron and has "liked" the Library's page)
- Either a computer for each participant, or one plugged into a projector so participants can all see the same thing
- Note taking materials (optional)
- Summary sheet of the sites discussed (optional)

**Prep Time:** Minimal – ½ hour depending on presentation format.

**Program Time:** An hour

**Number of Participants:** Will depend on format chosen, however it is more likely that a smaller group will keep the program on track.

**Number of Friends/Volunteers needed:** 1

**How/Notes:** If new sites come up and become popular, offer the program again or plan on conducting the program annually.

# #89 - Manage Investments

"Once I've invested my money, I'm done." Nope. Although managing investments shouldn't be a full-time job (unless you'd like to drive yourself nuts), it is a task that needs to be tackled from time to time. But, how often? And, what is the right balance in a portfolio? What does risk tolerance mean? What does diversity mean? These questions and more should be addressed in this program.

**Target Audience:** Adults - seniors

**Things needed:**
- An Instructor knowledgeable in investment management but not in the business of selling products. Recommend finding a recently retired banker or Certified Financial Planner
- Audiovisual support (if requested by the Instructor)
- Refreshments (optional)

**Prep Time:** Less than ½ hour to arrange space and set up audiovisual support.

**Program Time:** 1 – 1 ½ hours

**Number of Participants:** Limited only by space and Instructor's preference. Registration may be needed.

**Number of Friends/Volunteers needed:** 1

**How/Notes:** This program is best done in the half and half format. The Instructor dedicates half of the time to the presentation, then fields questions from the audience for the remainder of the time allotted.

Be open to the idea of follow on sessions if needed. It will depend on the depth of knowledge of the Instructor and attendees. Consider a Managing Investments 101 & 201.

# #90 – eReader class

I've long contended that each new electronic device purchased, should come with a 10 year old child to teach you how to use it. Obviously, that's not possible, but when my mom bought her Kindle, my son was the one she asked to help walk her through setting it up. She said there was a class at the library she planned on attending. The library? What a great idea! Coupled with the "how to" of the eReader, could also be instruction on how to access the library's eBooks on-line. This program would be fine as a stand-alone or as part of another series.

**Target Audience:** Seniors – anyone who needs help with their "gizmo."

**Things needed:**
- An Instructor knowledgeable with eReaders
- A librarian to demonstrate the process of checking out materials onto the eReader
- Audiovisual support (if needed)
- Refreshments (optional)

**Prep Time:** Minimal to arrange space, or up to ½ hour if the Instructor has a slide show presentation.

**Program Time:** An hour

**Number of Participants:** Try to keep this small, as multiple questions and hands-on work will slow down progress. Registration is recommended.

**Number of Friends/Volunteers needed:** None – the Instructor and library staff can handle this, unless offering refreshments, in which case, one volunteer will suffice.

**How/Notes:** Consider developing a good set of instructions with pictures and posting it out on the library's website. This might be a great project for the Teen Council, or as part of an inter-generational information exchange program.

Also include how to loan personally owned books to friends.

*"We live in the world of digital libraries. Print is fast becoming a memory. Despite this progression, the need for the library is more important today than in the past. Digitized information provides users faster, easier and more useful data than ever before." -*
*Deborah Peters*

# #91 – Safe driver program

The American Association of Retired Persons (AARP), sponsors a safe driver program, which is recognized by several major insurance companies. Participants who complete the course are provided a discount on their insurance. There may also be other safe driver programs that would benefit patrons, so find one that is reasonably priced and offer it as a program at the library. The whole community will benefit.

**Target Audience:** Senior drivers

**Things needed:**
- A Facilitator/Instructor
- Training materials
- Audiovisual support
- Computers
- Refreshments (optional)

**Prep Time:** Prep time is dedicated to finding and coordinating the Instructor, procuring materials and advertisement. Or, if only offering the on-line version, time to register participants. Additional minimal time to arrange the space for the program.

**Program Time:** 4 hours on average

**Number of Participants:** Limited to the number of computers available, if using only the online version.

**Number of Friends/Volunteers needed:** 1

**How/Notes:** A certificate of completion is issued 5-15 business days after completion of the AARP course.

If cost is a factor, consider offering to split the course fee with people interested in going through the course at the library. This will generate a commitment that will increase the likelihood of course completion.

*"Libraries store the energy that fuels the imagination. They open up windows to the world and inspire us to explore and achieve, and contribute to improving our quality of life. Libraries change lives for the better."*
*Sidney Sheldon*

# #92 – Genealogy tips & tricks

Tracing family history offers to be an enlightening and intriguing adventure. It can also be frustrating, especially when a "hot path" leads to a dead-end. Get folks together to discuss some sure-fire methods for searching family history including organization tips, free resources that are worthwhile and ideas for staying encouraged while weathering the unavoidable pitfalls along the way.

**Target Audience:** Seniors or anyone else interested

**Things needed:**
- A Facilitator – someone knowledgeable, perhaps the curator from the local historical society
- Audiovisual support to check out and display websites
- A list of good resources (optional)
- Refreshments (optional)

**Prep Time:** Minimal to arrange space

**Program Time:** 1 to 1 ½ hours

**Number of Participants:** Limited only by space and fire code

**Number of Friends/Volunteers needed:** The Facilitator is fine unless offering refreshments, in which case one volunteer is needed.

**How/Notes:** Make sure the discussion includes information about scams and how to avoid getting ripped off by people who pose as researchers, translators or validators of information.

# #93 – Local history trivia contest

Most communities have their life-long locals. A fun way to get them talking is to tickle their competitive side with a Local History Trivia contest. The format of the contest can vary – anything from a Jeopardy style game show to auction (everyone gets an A,B,C,D paddle or card and holds up their answer) to team Quiz Bowl with buzzers or even "Stump the Chump" where participants quiz each other.

**Target Audience:** Seniors

**Things needed:**
- A "Host" – consider a local historian (maybe the History Museum curator or Historical Society Director)
- Facts & questions related to the area
- Game cards (if needed)
- Space arranged for format chosen
- A timer
- Rules
- Refreshments (optional)
- Prizes (optional)

**Prep Time:** About ½ hour to set out refreshments if offering, and set up game and audience space.

**Program Time:** 1 ½ - 2 hours, but be prepared for the inevitable stories from the past. Guests may tend to linger. It would be best not to schedule anything else too close to the end of this program since it may run long.

**Number of Participants:** Players and audience will depend on the format chosen and the space available.

**Number of Friends/Volunteers needed:** 1

**How/Notes:** Possible side effects:

- Folks may bring in items for the Historical Society Museum
- More fun than the law allows

Advertising in the library should include a local history display in the game show format chosen.

This program could also be turned into a fantastic fundraiser with folks forming teams, getting sponsors and donating their proceeds to the library. Sell food at the event and raise even more money.

# #94 – Educational adventure travel

Architecture in Greece, archaeology in Mexico, geology darn near anywhere, educational vacations are a way for seniors to get up close and personal with knowledge they may have read about and have decided they would like to experience. The deeper use of the brain working into the higher levels of understanding aids in improving overall brain health. Share with participants some opportunities for educational adventure travel in this engaging program.

**Target Audience:** Seniors or anyone interested

**Things needed:**
- A Presenter
- Information
- Audiovisual support

**Prep Time:** Minimal to arrange space and set up audiovisual support

**Program Time:** An hour on the half & half format. ½ hour for presentation, ½ hour for discussion.

**Number of Participants:** Limited only by space and fire code

**Number of Friends/Volunteers needed:** 1

**How/Notes:** When making a Life list (Program #117), I'd be willing to bet that there is at least one, or in my case 3 dozen, desired trips in the future of list makers. So, mention the possibility of this program to folks during the Life lists program, to garner interest. *http://www.roadscholar.org/default.asp*

# #95 – Life circles – Writing prompts

This program is an excellent way to introduce the idea of leaving behind an autobiographical legacy for descendants. People tend to shy away from writing "my autobiography" because the project seems too daunting, or "my life just hasn't been that fantastic," or a myriad of other reasons that can only be described as "life got in the way." Some people leave behind journals, others do not, but their stories and thoughts are important treasures to their loved ones. Without the written word, some of those memories will fade very fast. There definitely are people who are interested in knowing about your life before them. "How did Grandma and Grandpa fall in love?" "When did you get your first car?" "Were the 50s, 60s, and 70s really like I see in the movies?" Get people together and present some every-day life writing prompts and see what happens. This program could be presented as part of a regular coffee chat, or as a stand-alone recurring program.

**Target Audience:** Adults

**Things needed:**
- An Instructor/Facilitator
- Some samples
- Writing prompts – a take-away sheet is a good idea, but be careful about copyright infringement
- Creativity exercises
- Paper, pens, colored pencils (for embellishment if desired)
- Refreshments (optional)

**Prep Time:** Minimal to arrange space

**Program Time:** 30 minutes to an hour each time, or an hour if only introducing and discussing the concept.

**Number of Participants:** Limited only by space and fire code

**Number of Friends/Volunteers needed:** 1-2, including the Instructor/Facilitator

**How/Notes:** Try these books for inspiration:

*The Story of a Lifetime* by Pamela Pavuk & J. Richard Huxen

*Take Ten for writers: 1000 writing exercises to build momentum in just 10 minutes a day* by Bonnie Neubauer

*Write Starts* by Hal Zina Bennett

*To our children's children* by Bob Greene and D.G. Fulford

Consider pairing up a writer who has difficulty writing with a student who can help by typing. This would be a great student community service project!

How about offering a book binding class at the end of the series? If the work went on weekly for 6 months, there would be a nice collection of at least 26 stories. What a tremendous gift for a family to treasure.

# #96 – Staying connected with far-away family

Long gone are the days when families tended to remain rooted in the same community. Now it is quite common for grandparents to have kids and grandkids across the country and across the world. Distance doesn't diminish love though, and this program is designed to inspire new connections and provide unique approaches to maintaining closeness across the miles.

**Target Audience:** Grandparents, parents, or families of deployed service members

**Things needed:**
- A Facilitator/Presenter
- Audiovisual support
- Reference sheet of ideas (optional)

**Prep Time:** Minimal to arrange space

**Program Time:** 1 hour

**Number of Participants:** Limited only by space and fire code

**Number of Friends/Volunteers needed:** 1

**How/Notes:** This program will work best as a presentation/discussion format. Present the idea and allow participants to expand on it and provide additional tips etc.

Talk about:
- The on-going story. Use email, mail, phone calls, etc. to write a story together. Decide on how much of the story will be produced each time, then surprise each other with new twists and turns!

- Pictures. But, not just any pictures. Depending on the age of the children, a travelogue of a treasured friend could be loads of fun. For example: A stuffed bear in our family has gone on several adventures and seeing the pictures is quite entertaining. Have the children send their treasured stuffie or doll or racecar to take their place with Grandma & Grandpa on their next outing and vice versa.

- A weekly phone call. We did this in our family. Grandma had a day designated for each kid and would call and talk to just that one each week. My kids were Tuesday and Friday, so when the phone rang on Friday, there was a VERY loud "I'll get it! That's Grandma calling for ME!" She talked exclusively to that child and all about "important stuff" like class work, soccer practice, Halloween plans etc.

- Reading. If you can't be there in person, how about providing a digital recording of a storybook, or reading via video chat?

- And speaking of video chat – video chat. But, caution! Kids lose interest very fast and should be encouraged to have things to show Grandma & Grandpa, like art pieces, lost teeth, favorite outfits, friends etc. And, don't expect the call to last long. A quick hello will be much more fun and anticipated if it doesn't go on too long.

- Make a family cookbook and include stories with the recipes.

- Grandpa's Advice for Life – send a weekly or monthly note with an age appropriate story of interest and a tidbit of advice to go along with it (dating, getting stuck in the mud, not making the team, goal-setting, overcoming "I got an 'F' on a test and now I'm not allowed to...", your Mom made mistakes too, let me tell you about the time...)

Remember! Remind participants when communicating with children, the fastest way to a dull conversation are questions with yes/no answers and questions that are too broad. "How is school going?" will get a quick "fine" or "okay" or, my favorite - "boring."

# Chapter 5 – Anyone and everyone interested - specialized

A "community of interest" is a group of people with shared interests and passions. The programs suggested in this section are designed for anyone interested and span a broader age range than those discussed in previous chapters. These programs will, in some cases, appeal to a specific community of interest or a more limited audience and will benefit from targeted advertising. Some of the programs are highly specialized and as you peruse them, you may think to yourself, "Yes! That sounds great – let's do this one!" A note of caution though: programs are time consuming to conduct and drain resources. Consider the demographic of the library, consult interest surveys, and be sure that there will be an audience before going to the effort of a specialized program.

*"A well-stocked, well-staffed library is like a gardener who plants books, knowledge, and dreams and grows readers, learners, and do-ers."Laura Purdie Salas*

# #97 – Cultural holiday celebrations

I recently had the distinct pleasure of celebrating Thanksgiving with some great friends and some new friends, of whom, one was from Korea and another from China. While we visited, the conversation turned to celebrations in those two countries. Thanksgiving, of course, is an American holiday rich in tradition, but what about other places? Look to the demographic of the community and seek to learn and celebrate more.

**Target Audience:** Everyone

**Things needed:**
- A Presenter/Facilitator
- A craft or food, depending on the holiday
- Games (optional)
- Music (optional)
- A video presentation (optional)

**Prep Time:** Will depend on the extent of the program

**Program Time:** 2 hours will be plenty of time to experience the traditions and have some activities

**Number of Participants:** Limited only by space and fire code

**Number of Friends/Volunteers needed:** Will depend of the size of the event

**How/Notes:** Consider the following as possibilities:
- Mardi Gras
- Chinese New Year
- Diwali (Festival of Lights)
- Summer Solstice

How about something each month?

> January – Jaipur Kite Festival (India) or the Harbin Ice & Snow Festival (China)

February – Carnival (Spain, Germany, Brazil)
March – St. Patrick's Day (Ireland, US)
April – Thai New Year (Thailand)
May – Cannes Film Festival (France)
June – World Cup Soccer (world-wide) or Festival of the Sun (Peru)
July – Calgary Stampede (Canada)
August – Obon Festival (Japan) or La Tomatina Festival (Spain)
September – Oktoberfest (Germany)
October – International Balloon Festival (US – New Mexico)
November – Day of the Dead Festival (Mexico)
December – New Year's Eve (world-wide)

Consider the food, dress-up stations, games, writing and crafts, as well as a visual presentation about the festival, its origins etc. Shh! Don't tell anyone it is educational fun.

# #98 – National "Who-sa-whats-it" month/week/day

My dad will be pleased to know that April 12^th is National Licorice Day (though he celebrates more often). When something is a national holiday... well, that is full license to enjoy to the fullest extent, right? Utilize some of these quirky "holidays" to do something special in the library and patrons will appreciate the display of whimsy. Build on already recommended programs, or see new suggestions below (How/Notes).

**Target Audience:** Everyone

**Things needed:** Will depend on the celebration

**Prep Time:** Also will depend on the celebration, though in most cases, minimal time and supplies will be needed.

**Program Time:** Once more, will depend on the program decided upon

**Number of Participants:** Will vary

**Number of Friends/Volunteers needed:** 1-2 for most activities

**How/Notes:** Here is a sample list of days that I think could be turned into interesting programs:

January
- National Handwriting Analysis Week: (19-25) Have fun with this one and sponsor a "What does your handwriting say about you?" program.
- 4^th - National Trivia Day. Host a team tournament. Theme could be anything from history to pop culture, to food or geography.

- 11<sup>th</sup> - Learn your name in Morse code. Cool drop in activity. Patrons can leave secret messages for each other. Be sure to have copies of the code for them to take home.
- 19<sup>th</sup> - Tin Can Day. Bring in full ones for the food pantry and do crafts with empty ones!

February

- National Entrepreneurship Week (3<sup>rd</sup> week) *http://www.entre-week.org/.* Tie-in to Business Plans (Program #48)
- 9<sup>th</sup> - Autism Sunday. Host an awareness event or fundraiser in honor of this growing body of disorders.
- 14<sup>th</sup> - Yes, it is Valentine's Day, but it is also Library Lover's Day. Show patrons a little love back by hosting a card making workshop.
- 18<sup>th</sup> - Cow milked while flying in an airplane day. I have no suggestions for this, I'm just wondering... What?! Who approves these things?
- 20<sup>th</sup> - Introduce a girl to engineering day. Love it! Do something special for your community girls on this day by hosting a How things work program (Program #4) just for them.

March

- Teen Tech Week (9-15). Make plans to update the webpage or social media pages.
- 3<sup>rd</sup> - Unique Names Day. Celebrate with a name centric art project. (This one is made in a Zentangle style Program #46)

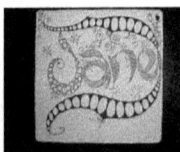

- 7<sup>th</sup> - National Doodle Day. Lay out a poster for patrons to doodle on, then frame it and hang it in the library for the month.

- 26$^{th}$ - Purple Day. How about using social media to offer $1.00 in Book Sale credit to anyone who comes in wearing purple on this day and asks? Do it a day or two in advance, or as a test of social media effectiveness, Flash Sale style.
- 26$^{th}$ - International Sister Cities Day. Celebrate your sister city library partnership (Program #171) on this day.

April

- National Public Health Week (First Full Week). *http://www.apha.org/programs/healthweek/* there is a theme each day.
- Global Youth Service Days (11-13). Projects can be done in the areas of Health, Education, Environment, Hunger, Community Building and Human Rights. Ever heard of a "Trash Mob?" Pick a place and get a whole bunch of people to clean it up quickly. Moss graffiti (Program #44), vertical gardening, sustainable fishing practices, plant trees, make blankets for kids or animals, go Orange for No Kid Hungry, host a SADD event, collect and donate kids dvds to Kid Flicks for pediatric hospital wards, build a Little Free Library in the community.
- 17$^{th}$ - Support Teen Literature Day. This would be a great day for a poetry slam (Program #68), or a book drive for teen material.

May

- Food Allergy Awareness Week (12-17) http://www.foodallergy.org/home. Tie into the Food Allergy series (Program #138)
- 1$^{st}$ - Lei Day. Make Leis, tell Hawaiian legends, and sample Hawaiian food.
- 12$^{th}$ - Limerick Day. Host a limerick writing workshop, or write one together throughout the day the library is open. Here is a funny one found on-line (no citation noted – author unknown)

> The Delinquent
> A delinquent who lived on his own
> Attempted to take out a loan.

When the banker said "no,"
The man asked with great woe
How his library fees had been known.

June
- Worldwide Knit (and crochet) in Public Week (9-17) *http://www.wwkipday.com/about* Invite local yarn crafters to an arranged spot at the library or on the library grounds.
- 15$^{th}$ - Nature Photography Day. *http://www.nanpa.org/nature_photography_day.php*
- 19$^{th}$ - World Sauntering Day. This would be a great addition to a Community weight loss program (Program #159), or Hosting a volkssporting event (Program #182) in honor of this day.
- 24$^{th}$ - International Fairy Day. How about tying in by doing the building a Fairy House program (Program #30)?
- 30$^{th}$ – Global Beatles Day. What better way to honor the Fab Four than having a Band Jam fundraiser (Program #188)?

July
- 7$^{th}$ - Father-Daughter Take a Walk Together Day. Host a walk and refreshments at the library. Perhaps a fun movie afterwards? How about *Father of the Bride?*
- 20$^{th}$ - Space Exploration Day. Have fun embracing all things space on this day.
- 29$^{th}$ - National Chicken Wing Day. Possible fundraiser here. Have a taste challenge contest and patrons pay to eat and vote. Split the pot with the winner.

August
- Weird Contest Week (Second Week). Go wild! How weird can you get? Recommend giving this to the Teen Council and see what they can come up with. Maybe a Book balancing contest with obstacle course?
- 14$^{th}$ – National Navajo Code Talkers Day. Honor these heroes with a history discussion. Expand into a series of folks who've risen to make a huge difference in our country.

- 3<sup>rd</sup> Saturday – International Geocaching Day. Introduce this new age Letterboxing (Program #118) by having a compass reading class and going out to find a geocache or two.

September
- Banned Books Week (Last Week). Set up a gorgeous display of some of these literary treasures.
- 10<sup>th</sup> - Swap Ideas Day. This would be a great day to get everyone together to do goal setting and program development for the upcoming year. Set out some refreshments and brainstorm away!
- 13<sup>th</sup>- Kids Take Over the Kitchen Day. Do a demo, talk about kitchen safety and give kids some tips on recipes they can make at home.
- 19<sup>th</sup> – Talk Like a Pirate Day. Have a pirate party!

October
- Financial Planning Week (1<sup>st</sup> Mon-Sun Week)
- Pet Peeve Week (2<sup>nd</sup> Week)
- First Saturday – World Card Making Day. Make blank cards to send to service members (Program #107)
- Wednesday of the second week - National Fossil Day. *http://nature.nps.gov/geology/nationalfossilday/activities.cfm*

November
- Geography Awareness Week (2nd Full Week) *http://education.nationalgeographic.com/education/collections/geographyawarenessweek/?ar_a=1*Consider things like how to use a compass, geocaching, letterboxing (Program #118), where in the world? (Hints to where something is located – first one with the right answer is the winner). Geography trivia game Family Feud or Jeopardy style.
- Health Information and Technology Week (2-8)

December
- Cookie Cutter Week (1-7) – How about a cookie cutter exchange?

- 17<sup>th</sup> – Wright Brother's Day. Have a paper airplane workshop (Program #25)
- 22<sup>nd</sup> – National Haiku Poetry Day. Have a workshop and artistically display the haiku.

I saw two seagulls
And a red bird in a tree
Waiting there for spring
      - Jennifer

# #99 – Cultural food experience

Have you ever tried....? This is a program that can take on many flavors. See what I did there? Ok, comedy isn't my strong suit. Anyway, cultural food experiences can be tied into standing nationally known festivals/holidays, like Cinco de Mayo, Chinese New Year or Oktoberfest. Or, they can be unique to the demographics of your area, or even serve as a rotating "Around the World with Food" monthly event.

**Target Audience:** Everyone

**Things needed:**
- A variety of books about the culture/festival being celebrated
- Audiovisual support (if needed)
- Great tasting food (Bonus if it is prepared by natives or descendants of the celebration culture)
- Recipe cards for the wonderful food
- Serving pieces
- Plates, napkins, utensils, cups
- Don't forget drinks!
- Music (optional but recommended)

**Prep Time:** About anhour to set-up, plus cooking time

**Program Time:** 1 – 1 ½ hours

**Number of Participants:** Limited only by the food and the fire code, but it will depend on whether the program is conducted inside, or outside; in a meeting room or not, and if the celebrated culture is well known in the community or not.

**Number of Friends/Volunteers needed:** Several for service, set-up and clean-up, or only one or two if the program is conducted as a small tasting event.

**How/Notes:** Decisions abound! Presentation could be a simple buffet, or the food could be presented as part of a travelogue presentation (Program #80), or have the food as part of a bigger festival. Your choice.

Recommend a speaker or slide show of photos from the celebration location. And, recommend including music, as it enhances the experience by layering in another of the body's senses.

*"A library is both comfort food and inspiration, opportunity for growth, and the place where anyone can come for personal enrichment. Judy Strong*

# #100 – Ways to help the community "go green"

There was a popular public service campaign in the 70s called "give a hoot, don't pollute" and it featured a cute cartoony owl who encouraged people to do their part to protect the earth. The library can pick up the baton and lead the way with a series dedicated to discussing ways to reduce the individual carbon footprint.

**Target Audience:** Everyone

**Things needed:**
- Presenters
- Information on the discussed topic
- Refreshments (optional)

**Prep Time:** Minimal to arrange space

**Program Time:** An hour each

**Number of Participants:** Limited only by space and fire code

**Number of Friends/Volunteers needed:** 1 to introduce the Presenter and handle refreshments, if offering

**How/Notes:** Recommend this as a monthly series and regularly soliciting ideas for more topics.

Ideas for starters:
- Community Supported Agriculture (CSAs)
- Off the Grid homes - try: *http://www.off-the-grid-homes.net* and *http://www.off-grid.net*
- Seed savers exchange (Program #175) try: *http://www.heirloomseedswap.com* and *http://www.southernexposure.com*
- Farmer's markets
- Eat locally - try: *http://www.eatlocal.net*

- Composting (Program #116)
- Volunteer for community clean-up days
- Waste-free lunch
- Hydroponic gardening
- eWaste solutions - try: *http://www.netplaces.com/green-living*

*"A library in the middle of a community is a cross between an emergency exit, a life raft and a festival. They are cathedrals of the mind; hospitals of the soul; theme parks of the imagination."* - Caitlin Moran, *Moranthology*

# #101 – Emergency preparedness series

Wildfires, tornados, hurricanes, earthquakes, blizzards, wide spread power outages and even volcanoes; the possibility exists of the need for an emergency kit. Every family will have different needs, so it isn't recommended that assembly of kits be part of this program, but donations of first aid kit components, dust masks, local maps, or emergency preparedness handbooks would make a nice addition to the discussion.

**Target Audience:** Everyone

**Things needed:**
- A Presenter (recommend the county Emergency Manager, Federal Emergency Management Agency (FEMA) representative or local Fire Chief)
- Audiovisual support (if needed)
- A list of recommended kit components (see How/Notes)
- The city's emergency response plan (or at least the citizen information and responsibilities part)
- Activities for kids for during the discussion (check with FEMA, or the local chapter of the Red Cross for coloring/activity books)

**Prep Time:** Minimal to arrange space

**Program Time:** An hour

**Number of Participants:** Limited only by space and fire code

**Number of Friends/Volunteers needed:** 1 to facilitate children's activities and introduce the Presenter

**How/Notes:** Consider including a sample house plan template that participants can use to work together to design their escape plans, understanding, of course that each house is different. Also, consider including a template emergency contact roster card participants can fill out and include in their kits.

*"A library outranks any other one thing a community can do to benefit its people. It is a never failing spring in the desert."* - Andrew Carnegie

# #102 – 100 best-of-all-time movies

Classic movies are classic for a reason – they are cinematically the best. This program can be presented at one per week in about 2 years; one every other week in a little over 4 years; do one per month and there will be a standing program for the next 8 ½ years!

**Target Audience:** Anyone interested (although many to most of the movies on the list are not suitable for children)

**Things needed:**
- The movies
- A projector & screen or digital player and monitor/tv
- Popcorn (optional, but a "must have" in my book)

**Prep Time:** Minimal to arrange space and set-up movie

**Program Time:** 2 hours approximately

**Number of Participants:** Limited only by space and fire code

**Number of Friends/Volunteers needed:** 1

**How/Notes:** Look at *http://www.thebest100lists.com* or *http://www.afi.com*

Add to the fun with movie trivia or a discussion of the film and its impact.

Add in periodic documentaries with follow-on discussions, or create a separate documentary series.

# #103 – Health & fitness series

As a follow-on, or in conjunction with the Community weight loss challenge (Program #159), this series is focused less on weight loss and more on overall health improvement through mind and spirit.

**Target Audience:** Anyone interested

**Things needed:**
- Instructors/Presenters – look to a yoga studio owner, naturalist, longevity specialist, whole healing and wellness center, aromatherapist, massage therapist, chiropractor, personal trainers.
- Audiovisual support (if needed)
- Reference sheets (optional but recommended)
- Other requirements will depend on the topic presented (see How/Notes)

**Prep Time:** Less than ½ hour to arrange space and audiovisual support if using

**Program Time:** 1 hour

**Number of Participants:** Limited only by space and fire code

**Number of Friends/Volunteers needed:** 1

**How/Notes:** Possible topics include, but are in no way limited to:
- Smoothies – make and taste
- Yoga
- Tai chi or Qi gong
- Pedometers and the benefits of a walking lifestyle. Discuss ways to sneak in extra walking time
- Ways to lower blood pressure
- Meditation
- Brain health activities (Sudoku, logic puzzles etc.). Couple this topic with a discussion on Alzheimer's disease.

- Smart phone apps designed to uplift, inspire, invigorate and motivate
- Gratitude journaling

*"Her library is a meeting place for all who love books. They discuss matters of the world and matters of the spirit."* - Jeanette Winter, <u>*The Librarian of Basra: A True Story from Iraq*</u>

# #104 – Conversational language series

Bonjour! Guten tag! Ni hao! How many ways in the world are there to say hello? Being able to order food, ask directions and read signs in a multitude of languages is something many people would like to be able to do while traveling. "Learn another language" is an item on many people's life lists (Program #117). A conversational language series could be designed for would-be travelers, or to connect segments of your very own community, or even to ensure the survival of an endangered tribal language, as is the case with the Menominee language of Northern Wisconsin and Michigan (according to *http://www.alsintl.com* there are only 39 first language speakers as of 1997). This program is a great stand-alone series, but could also be part of a travelogue series (Program #80) or other cultural enrichment series.

Target Audience: Ages 6+

Things needed:
- An Instructor – preferably a native speaker, but anyone with knowledge of the language
- A syllabus of intended topics for each class
- Audiovisual support (if needed)
- Refreshments (optional but nice to have them from the countries where the language being studied is spoken)
- The library's resources on the language and origin

Prep Time: Less than ½ hour to arrange space and set out refreshments.

Program Time: 1 hour

Number of Participants: Limited only by space and Instructor preference.

Number of Friends/Volunteers needed: 1 if providing refreshments, otherwise the Instructor can handle this program.

**How/Notes:** Have the Instructor provide a syllabus so there is assurance that the plan is consistent with the program goals.

This program can go in many different directions. It could be:
- A different language each time
- A weekly series with one language highlighted for 8 weeks or so, then switch to hit 6 languages a year
- A monthly workshop with a longer program run time (2-4 hours)
- Immersion style where hand gestures and internationally recognized symbols are used but only the chosen language is spoken.

# #105 – Book clubs

Book clubs get people together – which makes them perfect in every way. Look at the needs of the community. Are people asking about available book clubs in the area? Define the target group (Teens, seniors, women, men, 7th grade boys, 4th grade girls, Science Fiction, Westerns, General fiction). No matter which group comes, look for a welcoming space in the library for a rousing literary discussion!

**Target Audience:** Anyone interested

**Things needed:**
- A Facilitator
- A book – check with the library system – many systems offer book club "kits" which are tubs that include several copies of the book, along with a discussion guide, or set of book club questions.
- A timeline – most book clubs are successful with a once a month timeline, but some folks are so busy they prefer an every other month timeline.
- A discussion guide
- Refreshments (optional)

**Prep Time:** Minimal to arrange space

**Program Time:** An hour is good for a book discussion

**Number of Participants:** Less than 10 is ideal for a book club. If more than 10 are interested, consider breaking down further, or offering another session.

**Number of Friends/Volunteers needed:** 1 if offering refreshments, otherwise the Facilitator can handle this program.

**How/Notes:** Consider choosing a night in the week and offering different book clubs on different days (1st Wednesday is General

Fiction, 2$^{nd}$ Wednesday is Guys Read, 3$^{rd}$ Wednesday is 3$^{rd}$-5$^{th}$ grade girls, 4$^{th}$ Wednesday is Fantasy).

Or how about a book club week where each night is dedicated to a different group?

Decide how the club will be formatted and how books will be chosen. People like to know what to expect.

*"Entering a library is like entering a big cozy den in your home, where you may sit and read about anything, but it's also filled with friends." Julie Papievis*

# #106 – Knitting series

Knitting is a relaxing, yet rewarding craft. It is quite satisfying to hand craft and wear, or give something special. Plus, it is portable and easy to pick up and set down, which makes it a nice project for small moments of down time. Recruit a great volunteer Instructor, take it slow and soon the room will be filled with happy knitters. This program could easily branch out into a whole Yarn Arts Series.

**Target Audience:** Anyone interested

**Things needed:**
- An Instructor
- Donated or borrowed needles in a variety of sizes
- Yarn
- Scissors
- Patterns for participants to follow and take home

**Prep Time:** Minimal to arrange space

**Program Time:** An hour

**Number of Participants:** This program requires "hands on" guidance. Class should be small and limited to a number the Instructor feels comfortable supporting. Less than 8 participants is recommended for a beginning class.

**Number of Friends/Volunteers needed:** Instructor only, however, additional volunteers could assist more students, giving more flexibility to the class size.

**How/Notes:** Depending on interest, it might be more prudent to target the demographic more than "Anyone interested." Consider a knitting class for kids, seniors, or teens specifically.
Discuss different weights of yarn, the differences between synthetic and natural fibers, as well as appropriate applications for each type.

Cover needles – there are many different sizes, materials and shapes. What is used for what?

Cast on – discuss different methods and make sure that the Instructor covers more than one way to cast on. Everyone has a personal preference and the students should have a choice.

Once the instruction phase is complete, look in to sponsoring a knitting or yarn art circle, where folks just drop in with their projects. Or, have the circle at a follow-on time so that those needing instruction come for the program, then stay for the circle if they want to.

Thinking about a whole yarn art series? Crochet, weaving, felting, spinning, dying, latch hook are some options to consider.

# #107 – Decorative blank cards (donate to service men & women)

Many people love to write and send decorative cards and service men and women deployed overseas or recovering at a veteran's facility are no different. Turning blank card stock into decorative masterpieces is a fun and rewarding thing to do, but sometimes more cards are made than needed. This program aims to make _way_ more cards than are needed. Participants will make cards specifically to send to service men and women, so that the service members may, in turn, send the unique creations to their loved ones.

**Target Audience:** Everyone

**Things needed:**
- A Facilitator
- Card making materials (blank cards w/envelopes, decorative papers, scissors, glue sticks or dots, paper punches, ribbons, rubber stamps, stamp ink, tissue paper, stickers, markers)
- Some pre-made samples for inspiration
- Any available library resources for inspiration

**Prep Time:** Less than ½ hour to lay out the materials

**Program Time:** Can be drop-in for a 2 hour window, or a station at a larger event.

**Number of Participants:** As many as can be comfortably accommodated at the available space.

**Number of Friends/Volunteers needed:** 1-2

**How/Notes:** Contact a local veteran's organization, military base or possibly a recruiting office to get addresses for units deployed overseas. Or, contact the local regional Veteran's Affairs office for addresses of recovery centers.

Try setting a goal of a certain number of cards and let the group try to achieve it. Make a progress board and keep track of the total produced to up the fun factor.

*"A library is... liberty." Ann Patchett*

# #108 – Craft – Make & donate – pillowcase dresses

A friend of mine made these dresses with her church group to send overseas to developing countries. I've also seen versions on internet crafting sites. A work crew could whip out several of these dresses for kids in the community to enjoy all summer.

**Target Audience:** Anyone interested – there are jobs for helpers ages 5+

**Things needed:**
- An Instructor/Facilitator
- Pillowcases (need to be clean, but need not be plain)
- A variety of ribbons or bias binding (each dress needs about 60")
- 1/2" wide elastic (each dress needs about 12")
- Safety pins (use to thread the binding or ribbon through the casing)
- Scissors
- Fabric glue or seam binding
- Decorative accents (rick rack, ribbon, buttons, grommets) and fabric paints
- Sewing machines

**Prep Time:** Up to an hour to arrange workspace and set up stations

**Program Time:** 2 hours (or 4 hours as a drop-in program)

**Number of Participants:** Limited only by space and materials

**Number of Friends/Volunteers needed:** Will depend on the space, number of machines and participants supported. Recommend a ratio of 6-8 participants for each volunteer.

**How/Notes:** Arrange cutting, sewing, and decorating stations.

For this dress, the opening remains, and the folded end will be cut off and reconfigured into the neckline and arms of the dress.

1.  Cut off the top of the pillowcase. The amount cut off will determine the dress length. Consider a variety if this is a donation project.
2.  Cut a "J" shape at the sides for arm holes (come from the top so that the top seam is now narrower than the rest of the dress).
3.  Make a casing for elastic on the top edges, then use seam binding to bind the armholes (or thread ribbon through armhole casing) leaving long ends to tie over the shoulder.
4.  Decorate the bottom edge with rick rack, more ribbon, buttons or fabric paint

This could also be used as a cool fundraiser. Participants could pay a flat fee to make the dresses from materials provided. Or, the dresses could go up for silent auction.

# #109 – Astronomy night

I'm willing to bet that there is at least one amateur astronomer in the library's area who would be willing to come in and share their time, equipment, and enthusiasm and knowledge about the night sky with others. Use historical data to choose a probable starry night and gaze away – a planet or two may even be spotted!

**Target Audience:** Anyone interested

**Things needed:**
- An Instructor/Facilitator
- A few to several (depending on the size of the community and likely participation) high powered telescopes
- A clear night sky with something interesting going on in the sky (partial lunar eclipse, other planet visibility)
- A sky map (optional but recommended – try the app SkyView)
- The library's resources on astronomy and the night sky from both the reference and Juvenile reference sections.
- Stools or step stools to aid anyone who will need to be at a different height to see better through the telescope.
- Refreshments (optional, but wouldn't a warm drink be nice?)

**Prep Time:** ½ hour to an hour depending on format

**Program Time:** 1-3 hours, depending on format chosen

**Number of Participants:** Unlimited outside, but consider the number of telescopes available. It won't be much fun to come and have the line be so long, that some participants don't get a turn.

**Number of Friends/Volunteers needed:** 1-2

**How/Notes:** This program requires a back-up plan. In case of bad weather, either offer an information discussion about space, or cancel. Ensure that all advertising notes the plan for inclement weather and where to find the information (library webpage, social media post etc.)

Regardless of weather, it would be neat to have a slide show going on inside the library of what is possible to see, followed by questions.

Think about this. How about a whole "Library after Dark" night, with this as the centerpiece program? That way, if for some reason, the weather doesn't cooperate, there are still plenty of other activities available.

# #110 – Yoga

Yoga is an ancient spiritual Indian practice meant to attain a state of peace. Today yoga has been embraced by the west as a good form of exercise, increasing flexibility, core strength and yes, peace. Host a program to introduce yoga, show some basic moves and highlight its benefits.

**Target Audience:** Anyone interested

**Things needed:**
- An Instructor/Demonstrator – Look to a local studio or enthusiast. No formal instructor is needed
- A large flat space
- A few extra mats or beach towels
- Audiovisual support (if needed)
- Music
- A graphic of a few basic poses for patrons to take home

**Prep Time:** Minimal to arrange space

**Program Time:** An hour

**Number of Participants:** Registration will be required as there will be limited space.

**Number of Friends/Volunteers needed:** 1 (Can be the Instructor/Demonstrator)

**How/Notes:** Consider this program as an on-going offering, or target to specific demographics (parent/child night, seniors only, guys-do-yoga). Also, tie in to other recommended programs such as Healthy, wealthy, nifty & thrifty series (Program #76), Health and fitness series (Program #103), Community weight loss challenge (Program #159) or even Parachute play (Program #22).

- The tree pose – support yourself with strong roots

- The triangle pose – build a foundation of support
- The airplane pose – believe and soar!
- The fish pose – go with the flow and relax
- The lion pose – be brave and have courage
- The dog pose – be humble and accepting

For a program with kids try _My Daddy is a Pretzel – Yoga for Parents and Kids_ by Baron Baptiste

# #111 – Music appreciation series

Mozart to Maroon 5, Bach to The Beatles and Elvis to
EminEm. Throughout time music defines generations and
serves as a voice of the era. This series aims to compare and
contrast musical styles and break down music pieces while
seeking to appreciate them on their merits. Bask in the
pleasure of listening to music and seeing it beyond just the
notes and rhythms.

**Target Audience:** Anyone interested

**Things needed:**
- A Facilitator/Instructor – Embrace professional and
  novice music enthusiasts by asking for volunteers.
- Audiovisual support
- Additional music player (if needed)
- Note-taking material
- Refreshments (optional)

**Prep Time:** Minimal to arrange space

**Program Time:** An hour

**Number of Participants:** Registration recommended. Too
many participants and the joy gained from listening to and
discussing the music, may suffer. The number will depend on
interest and space available.

**Number of Friends/Volunteers needed:** 1

**How/Notes:** Use the following questions as samples:
- How are these two pieces of music similar/different?

- What life or cultural influences seem to have affected the song-writer?
- What are 3 words you'd use to describe the pieces?
- How did the rhythm of the music affect the mood of the listener?

That's just for starters. Let the Facilitator/Instructor build their questions based on the pieces they'll use in their presentation.

Be sure to include a discussion on the political climate and historical events of the time that may have influenced the song-writer (John Lennon's *Imagine* is a classic example)

Also, include international music that isn't as mainstream accessible.

# #112 – Drawing for beginners

If you've ever held a pencil, you've drawn, of course. But, to learn the elements of line weight, shading, perspective, depth and positioning is quite another thing. Host an introductory class or a whole series dedicated to drawing techniques.

**Target Audience:** Anyone interested

**Things needed:**
- An Instructor – Look to the high school art department or a local artist
- Audiovisual support (if needed)
- Easel with butcher paper (if needed)
- Scratch paper
- Quality paper
- Pencils, pens, colored pencils
- Artist erasers
- The library's resources on the topic
- Still life options or art pieces to duplicate
- Music (optional)

**Prep Time:** Minimal to arrange space

**Program Time:** 1 – 1 ½ hours. Run on the half and half format - ½ the time to discuss and demonstrate the concepts and techniques and ½ the time to work.

**Number of Participants:** Registration recommended. Everyone will need space to work. so limit to the space available and Instructor preference.

**Number of Friends/Volunteers needed:** 1

**How/Notes:** Discuss the following:
- Mediums: graphite pencils, charcoal, pen & ink, chalk, pastels, markers

- Support materials: paper, cardboard, plastic, canvas, leather, slate
- Strokes: hatching, cross-hatching, broken lines, stippling
- Visual impacts: dimension, proportion, perspective, depth, size, texture
- Techniques: erasers, rubbings, water, shading

This is meant to be an introductory program, but if interest endures, consider adding advanced classes, or dedicated time for patrons to come in and draw. If participants or the Instructor are willing to draw in open space where others can watch, that may serve well to gain interest in the program.

# #113 – Origami

Origami is the Japanese art of folding paper. It is intriguing to see completed projects and know that that beautiful piece of are is "only" folded paper. Amazing. Folks love to learn the art, so bring in this program to delight, entertain and educate.

**Target Audience:** Everyone

**Things needed:**
- An Instructor
- Origami paper
- Instruction sheets
- Practice space
- The library's resources on the subject

**Prep Time:** Less than ½ hour to arrange space

**Program Time:** 1 hour

**Number of Participants:** Recommend registration to ensure there is enough work space for everyone.

**Number of Friends/Volunteers needed:** 1

**How/Notes:** This program would work well as a drop-in or as a station at a larger event like the Library birthday party (Program #180) or Art show (Program #192)

Also available:
_Easy Origami_ by Didier Boursin
_Easy Dollar Bill Origami_ by John Montroll

Be patient! This class will have people of all ages, so make sure to have projects available for all ages and abilities.

# #114 – Chef demonstrations

New foods and new cooking techniques and gadgets are fascinating to people. Folks line up to watch demonstrations at fairs even if they have no interest in the product being shown. Why? Because food is life and life is fun! This program is meant to introduce new foods and new cooking techniques to the community.

**Target Audience:** Everyone

**Things needed:**
- A dynamic Presenter
- A microphone or microphone headset for the Presenter (if needed)
- Table (preferably elevated)
- Power source
- A hotplate
- An overhead mirror (recommended) or overhead projection (camera and projection screen)
- Recipe cards (optional but recommended)
- Plates, napkins and utensils for sampling

**Prep Time:** About an hour to arrange space and prep food

**Program Time:** An hour (time will be split between actual demonstration and questions)

**Number of Participants:** A small group is better, so registration is recommended.

**Number of Friends/Volunteers needed:** 1-2

**How/Notes:** Consider tying this program into a cultural food experience (Program #99), the Health and fitness series (Program #103), the Food allergy series (Program #138), National Who-sa-whats-it month/day/week (Program #98) or the Healthy, wealthy, nifty and thrifty series (Program #76)

Consider specializing and dedicating the series to comfort foods lightened up, or restaurant favorites you can make at home. Maybe combine this program with Meatless Monday (Program #146).

No matter the format chosen, participants will enjoy watching someone else do the cooking!

It is helpful to have samples ready ahead of time, as well as offering the recipes for participants to take home.

It may be required to get permission from the Fire Department, as the sensors on the sprinkler system may be too sensitive for cooking. Check first.

# #115 – Rubik's cube® demonstration & discussion

Rubik's cube® took the world be storm in the early 80s. And, it's designer, Erno Rubik, continued to develop and engineer challenging games like the Slide Cube and Rubik's 360. I got this idea from a friend of mine who used to own the book store in town. Her son was featured in the paper for his speed Rubik's cube® solving prowess and participation in competitions. I suggested she host a demonstration at the store, since my son was impressed. Of course, then ding! Another awesome library program idea. There is probably a local Rubik's cube® expert hiding in plain sight. Find that local expert and ask them to energize patrons into a new look at an old favorite.

**Target Audience:** Everyone

**Things needed:**
- A Demonstrator (if you can't find one, there are plenty of demonstration videos on *http://www.youtube.com* and the official Rubik's website, *http://www.rubiks.com*
- Audiovisual support if using websites as the Demonstrator
- Some Rubik's cubes and other games if people have them
- Refreshments (optional)

**Prep Time:** Minimal to arrange space

**Program Time:** An hour

**Number of Participants:** Limited only by space and fire code

**Number of Friends/Volunteers needed:** 1 to introduce Demonstrator and handle the refreshments if offering.

**How/Notes:** Gather participants around the demonstrator so that everyone can see.

Overhead mirror or camera and projection systems are good options if available.

*"Libraries are reservoirs of strength, grace and wit, reminders of order, calm and continuity, lakes of mental energy, neither warm nor cold, light nor dark ... In any library in the world, I am at home, unselfconscious, still and absorbed." – Germaine Greer, <u>Daddy, We Hardly Knew You</u>*

# #116 – Composting

Composting has come a long way in the "hip" factor. Long gone are the days when composting was a stinky, bug ridden pile in the back yard, inviting vermin and scaring away neighbors. Today's composters have decorative containers and lush gardens. So, host a program to talk about composting. What it is, the benefits, and how to do it yourself.

**Target Audience:** Gardeners and anyone else interested

**Things needed:**
- A Presenter/Instructor
- Audiovisual support (if needed)
- A list of resources (optional)

**Prep Time:** Minimal to arrange space

**Program Time:** An hour

**Number of Participants:** Limited only by space and fire code

**Number of Friends/Volunteers needed:** 1

**How/Notes:**
So what is it? Composting is the piling of green and brown organic material in a bin or ventilated container and allowing the material to rot or compost, while periodically turning to aid in breakdown. Once the material breaks down sufficiently, it is applied to a garden. The microbes and decayed organic material help enrich the soil by building up the health of the soil. When a garden has healthy soil, plants thrive as they utilize the additional nutrients provided in the compost. Composting is a popular way of making an organic supplement for the garden, and many experienced gardeners are now teaching composting to other gardeners and schoolchildren.

Composting can easily be a stand-alone program, or consider developing a gardening series (Program #137), or tying into a ways to help the community "go green" series (Program #100).

Many schools are joining the wave of composting and selling the compost to support their programs. Perhaps there is a potential partnership in there somewhere?

*"If you have a garden and a library you have everything you need." Cicero*

# #117 – Life lists

Some people call it a "bucket list," but a life list is a list of simple to elaborate, broad to specific, close to far-flung things that the list maker wants to experience in their lifetime. The great thing about a life list is ANYONE can benefit from the experience. Short and long-term goals can be included. A child might put "learn to tie my shoes" and "visit China" on the list and they both fit perfectly. This is a really fun program! It is also fun to have everyone share a few items on their list, if they'd like.

**Target Audience:** Everyone

**Things needed:**
- A Facilitator to introduce the idea and talk about the project
- Life Lists should be as personalized as possible, so an assortment of papers, stickers, markers and colored pencils will help get the creative juices flowing
- Samples, ideas (there are many resources on-line for ideas)
- Space for participants to brainstorm, look at samples and create their lists

**Prep Time:** ½ hour to set out supplies and arrange space

**Program Time:** 1 ½ hours. Once the idea is introduced participants will need time to work on their lists.

**Number of Participants:** If the space is small, reservations are recommended. Or, pre-make booklets and participants can take the booklets with them, which would allow for more participants (the format would change over to presentation with a take-away and no active work on the project in the library).

**Number of Friends/Volunteers needed:** 1-3

**How/Notes:** Lay out the materials, introduce the idea, share a few samples, and then let participants go wild documenting their life's desires. Move among them making suggestions ("Have you considered people you'd like to meet? Are there changes you'd like to make in your community? Do you build things?")

Remind participants that a Life list is just that – a list of dreams and goals for your whole life. Tastes and priorities change, there are introductions to new experiences which may lead to a completely new path. A few years ago, after trying to catch butterflies for a Department of Natural Resources project to tag butterflies and track their migration, I coined this phrase "That's the coolest thing I never knew I wanted to do!" Stay open to new ideas, and a fluid life list helps, I think.

# #118 – Letterboxing

Hide one in the library! Letterboxing is geocaching's Aunt Mabel. Much more low-tech and old fashioned, but just as fun. Where geocaching uses handheld GPS and coordinates, letterboxing uses clues and directions. Sometimes the clues are very straightforward, and other times very cryptic, like riddles which you have to solve in order to put yourself on the right path. Noted on *http://www.atlasquest.com* is the following: "The year was 1854, and a Victorian guide named James Perrott placed a bottle in the wildest, most inaccessible area on Dartmoor, England, along the banks of Cranmere Pool. In it, he included his calling card so future visitors could contact him and leave their own calling cards. Little did anyone know, this small act would become the hobby we now know as letterboxing."

**Target Audience:** Everyone

**Things needed:**
- A Manager. Someone will need to keep the box attended to and the website updated when necessary. The time commitment for this person is minimal.
- A box. If the letterbox is going to be in the library, a weatherproof box is not necessary. If the box is going to be placed outside on the library grounds, a small weather resistant, sealable container is needed.
- A stamp. Most stamps are handcrafted from artist's erasers or small blocks of wood.
- A log book and pen. Participants log their find in the logbook and place the box's stamp print in their book (like a passport book). Letterboxers typically carry their own logbook, stamp & stamp pad.
- Clues – check out *http://www.letterboxing.org* for ideas

**Prep Time:** Initial set up, then periodic monitoring/updates

**Program Time:** This is a drop-in and find it program. Or, there could be an introduction program first, then have the hunt, in which case, an hour is sufficient. 30-45 minutes for introduction and questions, then 15 minutes to find and log.

**Number of Participants:** No limit as this is an on-going program

**Number of Friends/Volunteers needed:** 1

**How/Notes:** Recommend that the Teen Council manage the letterbox and include how many times it has been found in the annual newsletter.

It also might be fun to make the letterbox a little less than super-secret. Post a tally board and write the names of those who have found the box. At the end of the month or quarter, draw for a prize (maybe a set of stamps, stamp ink, or logbook)

Include in the presentation a list of other clues in the local area. Consider re-hiding the letterbox every year or so.

# #119 – Craft – Paint book ends

A colorful library, decorated with patron art creates a sense of ownership unparalleled. My opinion of course, but I sure do like coming to the end of a row of books and seeing "my" book end. This craft is best as a drop-in program, part of an event or as a follow-on activity after Story Time.

**Target Audience:** Everyone

**Things needed:**
- The library's metal book ends
- Acrylic paints and brushes (plus cleaning water)
- A work space and a drying space
- Newspaper or drop cloths for the work surface
- Clear sealing spray paint (this part can be done later) which comes in gloss or matte finishes

**Prep Time:** About ½ hour to prep the space and lay out supplies

**Program Time:** It only takes 5-10 minutes to complete a book-end. Some folks might want to do several. How many there are available will determine the length of the program. A two hour window for drop-in, 30 minutes at the end of Story Time, or as a station the length of an event.

**Number of Participants:** Determined by method chosen and supplies available

**Number of Friends/Volunteers needed:** 1-2 depending on how many participants are accommodated at a time.

**How/Notes:** Instruct participants to NOT paint the bottom of the book-end (the paint will chip off quickly on the shelves and will hinder drying).

- Lay out the supplies (paint, paint brushes and water)

- Watch participants create fun, eclectic, masterpieces
- Once the pieces are dry, spray paint with clear sealer and allow to dry again.

If using this program as part of a larger event, recommend either the Library birthday party (Program #180) or the Sidewalk chalk art contest (Program #187).

*"A library is not simply a repository of books, it is the symbol and center of our culture - a door and a window for those who might not otherwise have such doors and windows." Amy Tan*

# #120 – Volunteer matching (speed dating for families)

Ok, I'm just going to say it... This is one of the coolest ideas I've ever had. It is possible that I didn't think of it first, and if that's the case, my apologies go out to the originator. Anyway, this program is a play on speed dating. The concept is simple – people meet for a few minutes on the auspice that they can get a real sense of whether they may be right for each other in a very short period of time. This can work for volunteerism too. Put the call out (recommend using the Chamber of Commerce for a complete list) to non-profits in the area that can use families as volunteers. Some groups can only accept help from adults, or the work available is not suitable for children. Thanks, but no thanks this time. An "adults only" session could be conducted another time, but families are the focus for this program because there are fewer opportunities for whole families to work together in a volunteer setting.

**Target Audience:** Families with children ages 6+

**Things needed:**
- A Facilitator
- Interested families
- Non-profit organizations with opportunities for families to help
- Seating arrangements for families and volunteer organizations with a table for table top presentations
- A timer
- Music (optional)
- Refreshments (optional but recommended)

**Prep Time:** Prep time is dedicated to arranging space and setting out refreshments + soliciting volunteer organizations to participate.

**Program Time:** 1 – 1 ½ hours. With 6-8 families and organizations, time frame is as follows: 5 minutes for presentation, 3 minutes for questions/discussion, and 2 minutes for transition. 6 participants = 1 hour, 8 participants = 80 minutes.

**Number of Participants:** Registration is essential for this program so that everyone is provided with an accurate sense of what to expect. If there are more families than organizations, set the organizations as static stations and rotate the families in volleyball style and vice versa.

**Number of Friends/Volunteers needed:** 1-2

**How/Notes:**
- Place families at tables spread throughout the library if there isn't a meeting room. If there is a meeting room available, try and achieve as much space as possible between tables to avoid conversation bleed over.
- Presenters move from table to table at the time keeper's signal
- Presenters may provide materials, volunteer opportunities, hours, and an overview of what they do and who they serve; anything that will give the families an idea of what would be expected of them if they chose to volunteer for that organization.

This program is meant to be fun, so think about including some fun transition music.

# #121 – How to use the library

Libraries have moved so far past fiction, non-fiction, periodicals and reference. Card catalogs are gone, as is the stereotypical "shhh." Libraries now have more resources than you can even lay your hands on. Now, more than ever, is the time for a 'How To' class. Even seasoned library patrons will learn something new from this program.

**Target Audience:** Anyone interested

**Things needed:**
- An enthusiastic, knowledgeable library staff member
- A list of services provided (It would be nice if this is done as an attractive graphic. Laminated, tri-fold, decorative – whatever, just make sure to include the library hours)
- Audiovisual support (if needed)
- Map of library (optional, but may be necessary for large libraries)
- Refreshments (optional)

**Prep Time:** Minimal to arrange space

**Program Time:** Up to an hour. Will depend on the size of the library, extent of the services provided and resources available, the size of the group and the number of questions asked.

**Number of Participants:** Registration recommended. It is important to have an interactive experience. Participants should be less than 8-10.

**Number of Friends/Volunteers needed:** 1 if offering refreshments

**How/Notes:** Consider a "Basic" and "Advanced" version of this program. Also, if there were a theme suitable to the library, then the experience could be done tour-guide style.

Entertain the idea of adding in a sneak-peek behind-the-scenes portion of the program. It doesn't really have much to do with how to use the library, but everyone loves to see what is usually an 'off limits' area.

*"When I got [my] library card, that was when my life began."* — *Rita Mae Brown*

# #122 – Identity theft

Yes. It can even happen to the dog. Identity theft is so pervasive that most everyone knows someone who has had to deal with the mess of restoring their credit and identity. Focus this program on the 3 D's – Deter, Detect and Defend. Enlist the local police department fraud unit to conduct this program. If they aren't available, there are ready-made presentations and promotional materials at *http://ftc.gov/idtheft*

**Target Audience:** Anyone interested

**Things needed:**
- A Presenter
- Audiovisual support
- Flyers or "tip sheets"

**Prep Time:** Minimal to arrange space

**Program Time:** An hour (30-45 minutes presentation, 15-30 minute question and answer)

**Number of Participants:** Limited only by space and fire code

**Number of Friends/Volunteers needed:** 1 to introduce Presenter and manage promotional materials

**How/Notes:** Make sure to have some coloring sheets or activities for young attendees to stay occupied.

For local statistics check *http://ftc.gov/sentinel*

Think about asking someone form a local bank or credit counseling agency to talk about the credit restoration piece of identity theft, which will add some depth and length to the program.

# #123 – Personal finance

This book is not about politics, so I will state simply that knowledge of personal finance is vital in building the blocks of responsibility and financial self-reliance. The library can be a great partner to people as they build a good financial foundation. Recommend this program as a series.

**Target Audience:** Anyone interested

**Things needed:**
- An Instructor/or Facilitator with discussion points – look to local experts and be mindful of the rules about soliciting within the library
- Audiovisual support (if needed)
- Budget Sheets
- Practice checks
- Calculators (optional)
- The library's resources on the topic
- Refreshments (optional)

**Prep Time:** Minimal to arrange space

**Program Time:** An hour

**Number of Participants:** Registration recommended to ensure an adequate amount of supplies. Or, if no supplies are utilized, there will be no need to limit the number of participants.

**Number of Friends/Volunteers needed:** 1

**How/Notes:** Recommend the following topics for consideration:
- Budgeting
- Compound Interest discussion
- Internet security (online banking and shopping)
- IRAs and other investment vehicles
- Ways to cut corners on spending when needed

- Insurance (needs vs. rip-offs)
- Credit Score (how to get it, what to do to improve it)
- Investing for the future
- Needs vs. wants
- Real Estate Investments
- Getting the best deals – shopping throughout the year
- Couponing (Program #152)
- Check writing and balancing the checkbook

This series could be developed for kids through coordination with Jr. Achievement, or a bank.

*"A library is richer than Fort Knox and everybody has the key." Robert Morgan*

# #124 – Community read and author/illustrator fan mail

Choose an author, boost up the library's collection with additional copies of the author/illustrator's work, then read together. What a great way to bring a community together!

**Target Audience:** Potentially everyone depending on the author chosen. Example – an author like James Patterson has a catalogue that extends to the elementary level; while an author like Alexander McCall Smith has an extensive catalogue appealing mostly to adults.

**Things needed:**
- A Facilitator/Event Coordinator
- More copies of the author/illustrator's work
- Opportunities to get together

**Prep Time:** Will depend on the event sponsored

**Program Time:** An hour each event

**Number of Participants:** Will vary depending on the event

**Number of Friends/Volunteers needed:** Will vary depending on the event

**How/Notes:** Many large systems have had great success with this concept.

Choose an author or illustrator with wide appeal or with local connections. Consider the following ideas as possible events:
- Get together and talk about the book, book club style
- Get together and celebrate the setting or food or era
- Do trivia games from the books
- Make a giant scroll as author/illustrator fan mail
- Have drawing events (learn to draw like...)

Polish the whole thing off with a party and hopefully a visit or video chat/message with the author/illustrator.

*"Amid the hectic pace of our lives, a library is like a comfy chair in front of a cozy fireplace on a wintry day, where people of every age and status can sit down and feel like they've come home... to a world without boundaries, to the world of books." C. J. Carr*

# #125 – Photography

This program requires a knowledgeable, enthusiastic and patient instructor. Learning some of the technical elements of photography will give participants a new perspective into this versatile art form. This program could easily be expanded into a technical series.

**Target Audience:** Anyone interested

**Things needed:**
- Instructor/Presenter
- Audiovisual support (if needed)
- Some static items to photograph (optional)

**Prep Time:** Minimal to arrange space

**Program Time:** 1 to 1 ½ hours

**Number of Participants:** Limit to less than 15 to maximize one-on-one time with the Instructor/Presenter - registration recommended.

**Number of Friends/Volunteers needed:** Instructor/Presenter can easily handle this program.

**How/Notes:** This is a hands-on program so participants should be encouraged to bring their own cameras.

Consider the following topics for this program and discuss the plan with the Instructor/Presenter:
- The basics – what do all of these buttons mean?
- Aperture
- Shutter speed
- Angles
- Exposure triangle
- ISO
- Composition
- Trick photography

- Distance/Depth
- Color modes
- Panorama and zoom (macro)
- Available editing software
- Lighting conditions

Use this program as an introductory pre-cursor to the Photography photo challenge and art show (Program #192).

# #126 – Craft – Rock and/or glass magnet

This project is relatively simple and really gets the creative juices flowing. Try it as a drop-in program, or as a project during another program. It can be a tiny bit messy and there is drying time required, so be mindful of that when deciding on program time and space dedicated to the activity. Think about possibly having Story Time or a book talk while the projects are drying.

**Target Audience:** Everyone

**Things needed:**
- A Facilitator
- Some finished samples (like the photo)
- Small (pre-painted) rocks with a flat side (for gluing the magnet to) or even pre-'magneted' so they are dry
- Clear glass beads (the kind used in vases – look at the discount or craft store in the silk flower section)
- Small round (strong) magnets
- Decoupage glaze (gloss or matte)
- Strong glue
- Scissors
- Decorative Papers
- Pencils for tracing around glass beads onto the decorative paper
- Letter stickers, or other small decorative stickers
- Fine tipped permanent markers
- Moistened wipes or paper towels for easy hand clean-up

**Prep Time:** ½ hour to lay out supplies plus time for shopping and painting. Note: for dark smooth river rocks, use white acrylic paint to give rocks a "primer" before painting with another color.

**Program Time:** 1 – 1 ½ hours

**Number of Participants:** Limited only by space and supplies. Note: These are very fun to make and participants will want to make several. If the supplies hold, provide 5-6 to start with, and let participants know that if there are leftovers, more will be available. Or, use pre-registration to be sure there will be plenty available for everyone.

**Number of Friends/Volunteers needed:** 1-2 depending on the size of the group

**How/Notes:** To keep projects aligned to the person who made them, recommend paper drying trays or towels. Participants should put their names on the trays so they can find their projects at the end. Anything that will contain the projects and can be written on will achieve the same result of keeping projects together.

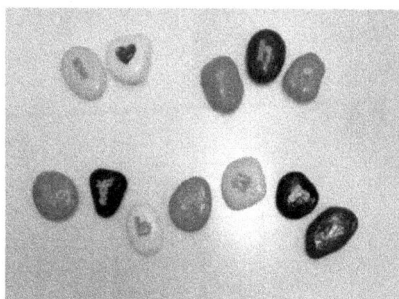

For the rocks:
- Gather, clean and dry, flat-bottomed rocks.
- Paint with acrylic paint. Let dry.
- Apply design (sticker or permanent marker, or both)
- Apply decoupaging glaze. Let dry.
- Apply magnet with strong glue.

*When painting the rocks, I've found that the easiest way is to finger paint. Fun and effective!

For the glass beads:
- Lay the glass bead over decorative paper (face up) and move around to look for desired design.
- Use a pencil to trace around the bead onto the paper.

- Cut out.
- Apply a very thin layer of decoupaging glaze to the bottom of the glass bead and position the picture. Let dry.
- Apply the magnet to the backside of the paper using a thin layer of strong glue that will dry clear and won't bleed through the paper.

*"The idea of a library full of books, the books full of knowledge, fills me with fear and love and courage and endless wonder."* - *Elizabeth McCracken*

# #127 – Craft – Beaded bookmarks

What makes a wonderful book even better? A homemade beautiful bookmark you either made yourself, or was given to you by someone special. This program will give participants the chance to make a few lovely bookmarks to keep or share. This craft can be conducted as a drop-in program, part of an event, or on its own.

**Target Audience:** Everyone

**Things needed:**
- A Facilitator
- A few finished samples
- Thin jute (it comes in natural and a variety of colors)
- Glass beads with holes big enough to feed the jute through, but not so big that they fall off after the jute is knotted at the end
- Scissors
- Small bowls to contain the beads (optional but recommended)

**Prep Time:** Will depend on the number of participants. Recommend pre-cutting the jute and making the initial knot to ensure proper length.

**Program Time:** An hour

**Number of Participants:** Depends on space and supplies available. The bookmarks go together quickly, so recommend having enough materials for everyone to be able to make 3-4.

**Number of Friends/Volunteers needed:** Little fingers will have trouble braiding and tying the knots. Depending on the demographic of the group, recommend 1 volunteer to support 3-5 children. Parents can fill this role, but at least 2 volunteers should be scheduled.

**How/Notes:**

- Cut 3 strands of jute approximately 18 – 21" long
- Tie a knot at one end, approximately 3 ½ -4 inches in.
- Braid the jute to the same distance from the other end and tie a knot. A tight braid will make the bookmark shorter, while a loose braid will retain length.
- String 3-5 beads on each string and tie off
- Trim ends to approximately ¼" from the knot.

This program could easily go into the fundraising section, as we've made them to sell. My daughter made them for a tiger habitat preservation project and also for our Relay for Life team. Since they are unique, they sold quickly.

# #128 – Craft –Book plates

It may seem strange to put on a program at the library for people to come and make book plates for their personal library collections, but participants can also make book plates for the library to use too. It is nice for libraries to acknowledge the generous book donations of their patrons – enter a pretty book plate! There are many resources on-line for printable book plate templates. I recommend printing some templates ahead of time, then the program can be either designing your own, or coloring in the pre-printed plates.

**Target Audience:** Everyone

**Things needed:**
- A Facilitator
- Some pre-made samples
- Templates (pre-print onto acid-free sticker paper)
- Acid-free sticker paper
- Printer
- Scissors or paper cutter
- An assortment of non-smearing, acid free markers or colored pencils (wouldn't want to ruin the book!)
- Work tables

**Prep Time:** About an hour to print and separate plates, set out supplies

**Program Time:** This can be an all-day event, used in conjunction with another event (a station), or be accomplished as a drop-in for a few hours. It could also be a follow-on or warm-up project for another program like the Fancy Nancy tea party (Program #26) or the Vision boards (Program #143).

**Number of Participants:** Limited only by space and supplies

**Number of Friends/Volunteers needed:** 1 + Facilitator

**How/Notes:** Make sure to use archival quality paper and markers. Markers need to be fast-drying and plentiful. Also include some font style sheets for participants to reference which will add some extra flair to their book plates.

*"I like libraries. It's a comfort that knowledge can be save for so long. That what we learn can be passed on."* - Jackson Pearce, <u>*Sisters Red*</u>

# #129 – Decoupage collage rocks

This project was proposed and presented by a volunteer. She brought all kinds of cut out pieces of fabric, wall paper and decorative paper. The Friends collected rocks and bought decoupage glaze. We had a rock painting party ahead of time, so that when patrons came in, all they had to do was select a rock, what they wanted to put on it, and start decoupaging. We also had paint and markers on hand to add writing if participants wanted. We polished off the pieces with clear lacquer spray paint to make them weather resistant. This project was done right before Father's Day and the race car rock my kids made, still resides in my dad's sunroom, six years later.

**Target Audience:** Everyone

**Things needed:**
- Medium sized river rocks (they need to be smooth and not so big that they can't be easily lifted, but large enough to get some good designs on them. Think door-stop sized)
- Acrylic paint – lots of it
- Decorative paper, fabrics, wall papers and stickers
- Scissors
- Markers
- Decoupage glue and containers to put it in (foam trays work well, as do small plastic containers like yogurt or margarine cups)
- Foam paint brushes
- Clear lacquer spray paint (fast-drying)
- Drying space

**Prep Time:** A few days. As mentioned in the introduction, a painting party to establish the base of the rocks is needed + acquiring and cleaning the rocks, as well as, prepping some decorative embellishments.

**Program Time:** Depending on the work space available and the number of rocks, this program may need to be run in two shifts. 3 hours total.

**Number of Participants:** Limited to the amount of supplies available. Registration recommended.

**Number of Friends/Volunteers needed:** At least 2

**How/Notes:** Consider an on-going story time or face painting or something to occupy participants while their projects are drying or they are waiting for work space to open up. Perhaps a book plate making station (Program #128)?

# #130 – Board-game tournaments

A board-game tournament is a fun twist on a card tournament. What's great about it is that depending on the games chosen, everyone, no matter how old, has a chance to win. Choose a few fun games that most people know, such as Sorry®, Chutes & Ladders®, Apples to Apples®, Monopoly®, checkers, backgammon, Clue® or Trouble®. This program could be turned in to a fundraiser if players and/or spectators are charged to play or watch and prizes are offered.

**Target Audience:** Everyone ages 5+, or specialized if needed

**Things needed:**
- A Facilitator/Timekeeper/Referee
- A variety of games (with established rules). *Note: Many games offer a variety of playing options, so make sure everyone knows which set of rules is being used before starting.
- A method of timekeeping
- A tournament bracket
- Prizes (optional)

**Prep Time:** About a ½ hour to arrange space and set-up games

**Program Time:** A two-hour time frame for the games should be sufficient, with a prize presentation at the end.

**Number of Participants:** Registration is recommended to ensure enough space and time for everyone to play. The number of participants will be determined by the space available and the number of games on-hand.

**Number of Friends/Volunteers needed:** 2+

**How/Notes:** Make sure to have a "Code of Conduct" and standardized rules for each game so there are no disputes.

Players could play in teams or for themselves. Tournament could be single elimination or play for points so that everyone gets to play the whole time, but the winner is determined by the number of points scored.

It is okay to have games that younger people don't know, as the program can be designed to make sure they are always playing a game that they do know.

Recommend a time limit for each game. Participants could switch to new games or rotate amongst a few tables of the same game.

# #131 – Comedy or acting improv workshop

Calling all would-be comedians and comediennes, actors and actresses! Even the most naturally funny and dramatic will enjoy working on their timing skills and trying to think on their feet at this program. It is hard to think in front of an audience. A workshop like this could benefit anyone who is interested in improving their "stage presence." From having to present a book report in class, to addressing the stockholders - improvisation can help anyone.

**Target Audience:** Everyone

**Things needed:**
- An Instructor/Facilitator
- Audiovisual support (if needed)
- A list of skills to be taught
- A list of improvisation exercises
- Some props
- Refreshments (optional)

**Prep Time:** Minimal to arrange space

**Program Time:** An hour

**Number of Participants:** Limit this program to less than 15 (keeps the noise down and everyone gets a chance to practice the skills), as well as provide good feed-back to each other. Registration will be required.

**Number of Friends/Volunteers needed:** 1 + the Instructor/Facilitator

**How/Notes:** This program would be fantastic as a 4-6 week series with a new skill presented each week.

Be prepared to conduct the workshop if the Instructor/Facilitator is unavailable. Look for clips from the television show *Whose line is it anyway?* and break down the brilliance of guys like Wayne Brady and Ryan Stiles.

Or, replicate some of the exercises from the show.

Preparedness is the key to the success of this program. Which is ironic isn't it? Since improv itself is all about winging it (with skill).

# #132 – Song writing workshop

What are the elements of a song? I hear things like 'melodies,' 'the bridge' and 'harmonies' and have only an inkling of what all that means. Host a song-writing workshop and help participants learn all the elements of what makes a great song, and what makes a song great.

**Target Audience:** Anyone interested

**Things needed:**
- An Instructor – Look to the high school music department or a locally famous musician for help
- Audiovisual support (if needed)
- The library's resources on the subject
- Music paper and pencils
- Keyboards (if doing as a series)
- Refreshments (optional)

**Prep Time:** Minimal to arrange space

**Program Time:** An hour

**Number of Participants:** Limit this to less than 10 participants. Registration will be required.

**Number of Friends/Volunteers needed:** 1

**How/Notes:** Try to offer this as a series in which participants commit to a 4 – 6 week course. Make sure to include the following:
- Melody
- Chords and chord progression
- Beat and rhythm
- Genre & style
- Concept (what is the story?)
- The "hook" (the part that sticks in your head)

- Lyrics
- The song sections (verse, chorus, bridge)
- Arrangement
- Selecting a key

*"Libraries are the soul of our country. We must nourish them so they can live with us forever."*
*Elizabeth Flock*

# #133 – Home remedies series

Commercial remedies are available for nearly any common malady regularly experienced by people. But many people don't like the idea of utilizing synthetic chemicals that can't be pronounced. Fortunately there are plenty of effective home remedies. Host a regular home remedy series once a month and give participants a chance to share what works for them.

**Target Audience:** Anyone interested

**Things needed:**
- A Facilitator
- Audiovisual support (if needed)
- A lesson plan

**Prep Time:** Minimal to arrange space

**Program Time:** 1 hour

**Number of Participants:** Limited only by space and fire code

**Number of Friends/Volunteers needed:** 1

**How/Notes:** Break down the series into categories like: cleaning solutions, brain health, weight, aches and pains, hair, men, women, seniors, kids, infants, pets.

Include topics such as:
- Migraines
- Bloating
- Back Pain
- Sore Throat
- Troubled Sleep
- Uneven skin
- Muscle aches
- Damaged hair

- Acne
- Psoriasis
- Acid reflux
- Anger
- Anxiety
- Blood pressure
- Cleaning products
- Hot flashes

Try *http://www.myhomeremedies.com* for more ideas.

Ask patrons via an on-going survey what they'd be interested in hearing more about.

# #134 – Skills demonstrations

Craftsmen who provide specialized instruction often look for opportunities to reach out to the community. Give them that chance by hosting a series of skill demonstrations in the library.

**Target Audience:** Anyone interested

**Things needed:**
- Willing, skilled Demonstrators
- Audiovisual support (if needed)
- Adequate space
- Great advertising

**Prep Time:** Will be dependent upon the Demonstrator's needs

**Program Time:** About an hour with 30-45 minutes dedicated to demonstration and 15-30 minutes for questions.

**Number of Participants:** Limited only by space and fire code

**Number of Friends/Volunteers needed:** 1 to introduce the Demonstrator and manage any survey collection.

**How/Notes:** Potential demonstrations suitable for the library:
- Karate
- Music (voice and instrument)
- Yarn spinning
- Beading
- Solder (check with the Fire Chief to make sure it is okay to do this inside)
- Basket weaving
- Cake decorating
- Pop-up cards
- Dance
- Photography

Local businesses cannot specifically "sell" in the library, but they can leave behind promotional material. Advertise the opportunity through the Chamber of Commerce rather than reaching out to specific businesses so that the library doesn't present the appearance of favoritism, especially if there is more than one provider of that type of service/skill in the community.

When advertising for demonstrators, make sure to include the capabilities of the space (size, power, length of program etc.).

*"I worry about how many children read. Libraries are more important today than when I was a kid. - John Grisham*

# #135 – Community knowledge series

A wonderful way to embrace the neighbors is to partner with them. Ask them to come in and share their expertise with program participants.

**Target Audience:** Anyone interested

**Things needed:**
- Community business people as Presenters
- Audiovisual support (if requested)
- Refreshments (optional)

**Prep Time:** Minimal to arrange space and set up requested audiovisual support

**Program Time:** An hour each

**Number of Participants:** Limited only by space and fire code

**Number of Friends/Volunteers needed:** 1

**How/Notes:** It is important to note that business owners cannot sell anything in the library, but are welcome to state where they are from and leave business cards, or promotional materials.
Ideas:
- The pet store owner to discuss pet health, pet nutrition, pet readiness
- The investment broker to discuss financial planning
- The dentist to discuss oral health
- The chiropractor to discuss whole health and the art of de-stressing
- The auto shop owner to discuss car maintenance and recommended services
- The mortgage broker to discuss home financing and credit scores

- The tax accountant to talk about new tax laws and ways to reduce your tax bill
- The radio station manager to demonstrate sound mixing and discuss radio programming
- The community theatre director to discuss the elements of putting on a community theatre production
- The music store owner/manager to do instrument demonstrations
- The hair salon owner to cover healthy treatment of hair and choosing a style that is complementary to your face
- The outdoor equipment store owner with survival tips or to discuss the area's recreational seasons
- A local realtor to talk about bang-for-the-buck home improvements and the local real estate market
- A local contractor to discuss necessary questions to ask contractors prior to embarking on a home improvement project

# #136 – Horse equipment demonstration/discussion

Majestic mysterious creatures and at some point, nearly all children (and lots of grown-ups) are totally enamored with them. Bridge the gap and help participants learn about horses and their tack.

**Target Audience:** Anyone interested

**Things needed:**
- A Presenter – Look to a nearby ranch, vet or enthusiast for a volunteer
- Horse 'stuff' – saddles, bridles, bits, reigns, blinders, blankets, stirrups etc.
- Audiovisual support (if needed)

**Prep Time:** Minimal to arrange space

**Program Time:** An hour

**Number of Participants:** Limited only by space and fire code

**Number of Friends/Volunteers needed:** 1

**How/Notes:** This program is best done as a "display & discuss" format. Have the Presenter lay out all the tack and discuss what it is and how it is used. Presenter should be prepared to answer a LOT of questions!

It is especially helpful if the Presenter brings items that participants are encouraged to touch, which enhances the overall experience.

# #137 – Gardening

Many people love gardening, or at least the idea of gardening. And, just as many people classify themselves as "plant killers" because, although they try, they just can't get their garden to thrive. A program about gardening would be best as a series, but could be specific too. Is there a particular garden pest in the area? Design a program for that. Is there difficult soil? Design a program that discusses great plants for the area's challenges. How about a series entitled *Gardening for the "Un" green thumb* with tips and tricks to keep plants alive? Think of clever program titles for the series like *The Lazy Waterer –Plants that are drought resistant*, or *Kill me not – Plants for those who think they can't garden*. What about natural solutions to pest control? The list goes on & on. Survey patrons or the local garden club for even more ideas.

**Target Audience:** Garden enthusiasts to anyone interested

**Things needed:**
- Presenter – try to find a master gardener or volunteer with gardening knowledge
- Audiovisual support for the presentation (if requested)
- Space to sit
- Refreshments (optional). Presenting a program about herbs? How about serving tea with lemon balm or mint?

**Prep Time:** Less than ½ hour to arrange space and set up for audiovisual support if needed

**Program Time:** Plan on an hour. Programs like this typically follow the half and half format. ½ hour for presentation and ½ hour for question and answer.

**Number of Participants:** Defined by space and Presenter preference

**Number of Friends/Volunteers needed:** 1, if offering refreshments, otherwise the Presenter can handle this program.

**How/Notes:** Most major universities have extension programs dedicated to gardening. Contact them for support in designing a great series, or providing a Presenter.

A good time to do a gardening series is starting a month or so before planting season and running part way into the growing season. A weekly or bi-weekly series for 2 ½ months would probably be well attended and get folks pretty excited about gardening.

Live in an urban area? How about a program on guerrilla gardening? Or small space, big yield gardening?

Tie in the Composting program (Program #116) to the series, as well as organic gardening.

Have a local food bank? Do they have a garden? Maybe patrons don't want to commit to a garden of their own, but would love to help out in a community garden. They could connect with each other at the library!

# #138 – Food allergy series

When I was first diagnosed with a food allergy, I had many more questions than answers. Through my research, a number stuck in my head. The common statistic quoted is that nearly 8 million Americans, or roughly 2.5% of the U.S. population has a food allergy. Discussion about why could go on for hours, but the goal of this series is to shed light on identifying, reacting to, and living with food allergies.

**Target Audience:** Anyone interested – especially people who are caregivers or who feed people

**Things needed:**
- A Facilitator – Recommend a community health nurse or dietician or someone who has a lot of experience with food allergies
- Audiovisual support (if requested)
- List of resources
- The library's resources on the topic
- Recipes

**Prep Time:** Minimal to arrange space

**Program Time:** An hour

**Number of Participants:** Limited only be space and fire code

**Number of Friends/Volunteers needed:** 1

**How/Notes:** Do this as a weekly series and repeat once a year or every other year, depending on interest.

Recommended series components:
- Discussion of the 8 major food allergens (Dairy, eggs, peanuts, tree nuts, fish, shellfish, soy and wheat)
- Identifying an allergy - signs to look for, questions to ask

- Epinephrine – how to, why to, when to and medical treatment
- Other life threatening allergies – stinging bugs, latex and others
- Communicating with teachers, friends, parents & caregivers
- Substitutes – great recipes which don't include the allergen
- Food preparation
- Eating out
- Reading food labels, including unintended ingredients – For example, I have a friend who is allergic to coconut. Simple right? Just avoid coconut. Wrong! Derivatives of coconut are usually, but not always, listed as palm kernel oil. Say what? Think about it. Coconuts grown on palm trees, so their nut (or kernel) is the coconut itself. And, palm kernel oil is used in a massive amount of products. She called me one day after an emergency room visit. "Did you know that Fanta® orange soda has coconut in it? I sure didn't, but I do now!"

# #139 – Metaphysical series

Exploration and discovery of the inner self, connection with nature and the heavens and all things "thought." This is what is defined as metaphysical science. Host a series to explore the many aspects of the metaphysical sciences.

**Target Audience:** Anyone interested

**Things needed:**
- Presenters/Speakers
- Audiovisual support (if needed)
- Graphic resource cards (if appropriate)
- Refreshments (optional)

**Prep Time:** Minimal to arrange space

**Program Time:** An hour

**Number of Participants:** Limited only by space and fire code

**Number of Friends/Volunteers needed:** 1 + Presenter/Speaker

**How/Notes:** Any one of these suggested topics could easily be expanded into its own series. Consider an exit survey to see which have a deeper interest level – or – do the survey before starting the planning for the series to see which topics patrons are interested in learning more about.

Possible topics:
- Philosophy
- Mysticism
- Dreams
- Astrology
- Meditation
- Reincarnation
- Positive thinking

- Extrasensory perception (ESP)
- Tarot
- Numerology
- Sensory articulation

*With a library it is easier to hope for serendipity than to look for a precise answer." - Lemony Snicket, <u>When Did You See Her Last?</u>*

# #140 – Turn off the TV week activities series

Turn off the TV week, or Screen-Free week is a national initiative aimed to unplug electronics and plug in to life, family and fun. This week, which has been embraced around the country, is a prime opportunity to get people into the library. Offer activities each night and enthusiastic new patrons will be back for more.

**Target Audience:** Everyone

**Things needed:**
- Facilitators
- A list of great activities
- Any needed supplies for chosen crafts, games or activities
- Refreshments (optional)

**Prep Time:** Will depend on activities chosen

**Program Time:** It is a Monday – Friday event during the school year, so an hour should suffice. Recommend a program time of 6:00-7:00pm (after dinner but still before bed).

**Number of Participants:** Limited only by space, fire code and supplies. Recommend registration if needed.

**Number of Friends/Volunteers needed:** Will depend on activities chosen

**How/Notes:** A few ideas suitable for families and the library:
- Cultural food experience (Program #99)
- Make and decorate a wooden flower box or birdfeeder
- Make a kite to take home and fly
- Make puppets
- Host skills demonstrations (Program #134). This will show young participants that there are many available activities in the community for them to try.

- Family art (Program #164)
- Family game night (Program #165)
- Create a giant collage to be displayed in the library (favorite things that aren't screens/television). This will show everyone that they have great things in their lives! Do this activity on the first night, so it will be a visual reminder all week!
- Cookie exchange or Cookies in a jar (Program #18). Then the family can go home and bake together.
- Have a poster design contest for Screen-Free Week
- Make cards to send to service members overseas (Program #107)

# #141 – Pregnancy, birth & beyond series

This multi-faceted series is designed to get information out to patrons and make connections between new parents and other new parents. It will also highlight the community resources available to parents as they navigate the unchartered waters of birth and parenthood.

**Target Audience:** Soon-to-be and new parents

**Things needed:**
- Dynamic Speakers/Instructors
- Audiovisual support (if needed)
- Reference sheets (optional)
- Refreshments (optional but recommended)

**Prep Time:** Minimal to arrange space

**Program Time:** 1 hour

**Number of Participants:** Limited only by space and fire code

**Number of Friends/Volunteers needed:** 1

**How/Notes:**
Pregnancy topic suggestions (many of these are covered in prenatal classes, so coordinate with local providers and try to cover areas that may not be addressed elsewhere):
- What your baby looks like along the way
- Massage
- Exercise during pregnancy
- Preparing for baby
- The benefits of music, different foods etc.
- Preparing siblings for baby

Birth topic suggestions:
- Doula, Midwife, traditional medicine?

- Natural birth options
- Communicating with loved ones
- How to handle complications

Beyond topic suggestions:
- Immunizations
- Infant CPR and other first aid needs
- Traveling with baby
- Baby-proofing
- Bathing and sleeping
- Breastfeeding

Gauge interest for other topics with an interest survey.

Make sure to note on advertising that there is no specific product endorsement to be implied by having various speakers.

It is possible that local providers may need to partner with someone for extra space for their prenatal classes. Perhaps the library is an option for more in-depth prenatal classes?

# #142 – Community history project

What do you know about the history of your community? If you are like me, the answer is "not as much as I should or would like to." In my local paper, there is an 'On this Date' section, which I like. But what do the patrons remember? This program aims to capture those memories and preserve them. Once complete, bind as a book for the library's collection.

**Target Audience:** Everyone

**Things needed:**
- A Facilitator/Guide
- A list of goals for the project along with desired outcomes (a bound book is just one option)
- Audiovisual support (if needed)
- Writing prompts (see How/Notes)
- Paper
- Timeline for completion

**Prep Time:** Minimal for the program, planning is a bit more in-depth.

**Program Time:** On-going for the duration of the project. Introductory program should be one hour.

**Number of Participants:** Hopefully everyone

**Number of Friends/Volunteers needed:** 1-2 to collect and edit or retype submissions

How/Notes:
This could be a year-long project or longer or shorter depending on how in-depth the undertaking and the age of the town. For example – a year a week = 52 years of history, but that is asking an awful lot from patrons and the product will lack in completeness and substance. A year per month will net 12 years of history and the

timeframe may result in a loss of interest. Recommend a five-year span every other week, and occasionally focusing on personal memories of a significant event (where were you when?) (How did 'event X' affect this town?)

Make sure that submission sheets include participants name and phone number so that the scribes can contact them with questions.

Consider partnering with the Historical Society for recommendations. The aim of this program isn't to produce an official town history, but rather a collection of personal memories to ADD to the historical society's collection.

Will photos be included? They should be. If they are, there may be a requirement for photo release forms, depending on the date of the photo.

What about video? Possibly. Will depend on the stated goals and parameters of the project.

Some possible writing prompts:
- In Pleasantville, in 1980, my family_____.
- 2002 was a good/bad year for Pleasantville because

  _____.

- Pleasantville was in the spotlight in 1970-1975 because

  _____.

- I remember the _____ business during the 1960's. The best/worst part about that place was _____.
- The most important community figure to me in the 1990's was _____. They _____.
- The day that _____ happened, I was _____. I remember feeling ____.

# #143 – Vision boards

_The Secret_ by Rhonda Byrne is one of many publications which touts the power of positive thinking. At my daughter's school a sign reads "If you believe, you can achieve." Many people believe that a vision board helps give focused energy and direction to the creator of the board. And, even if it is all hooey, the process is still fun and it is always nice to have pictures around that make you happy. Unlike the career interest program (Program #62), this program focuses on things (people, ideas, places etc.) participants want to have in their lives.

**Target Audience:** Anyone interested

**Things needed:**
- A Facilitator to introduce the idea and have a short discussion with participants
- A few samples
- Small poster boards
- A variety of magazines
- Scissors
- Glue sticks
- Markers
- Stickers & other decorative embellishments

**Prep Time:** About ½ hour to lay out supplies and arrange space

**Program Time:** 1 – 1 ½ hours

**Number of Participants:** Limited only by space and supplies

**Number of Friends/Volunteers needed:** 1-2 including the Facilitator

**How/Notes:** This isn't a sharing activity so participants should be instructed to work at their own pace and when they feel they are done, they can go. Or if there is interest, sometimes it is fun to share with others what you want for your life, just to hear it come out of your mouth. After all, that is the premise of asking the universe for what you want. The vision bard is made as a conduit for the energy.

The facilitator should complete a board prior to the event so they can share it in the introduction and provide some creative inspiration to participants.

A nice touch – have some great pictures and sayings already cut out

# #144 – Crafting

For this series the idea is to introduce different crafting genres. Present lesser known crafts to new crafters and highlight the library's resources on the topic to increase circulation.

**Target Audience:** Anyone interested

**Things needed:**
- An Instructor/Facilitator
- Audiovisual support (if needed)
- Plenty of workspace
- Enough supplies for everyone to have a chance to try
- The library's resources on the craft presented
- Basic instruction sheets with good website references (optional but recommended)

**Prep Time:** ½ hour to lay out supplies and arrange space

**Program Time:** 1 hour

**Number of Participants:** Keep the numbers down to less than 12. Registration recommended.

**Number of Friends/Volunteers needed:** 1 + Instructor/Facilitator

**How/Notes:** As crafts are introduced, take a survey or poll to see if any of the crafts are hugely popular. The crafts that create the most interest can be developed into a follow-on series incorporating more in-depth instruction, time to work clubs and potentially a fund-raising event for the library.

Some possible crafts:
- Macramé
- Wood carving/burning
- Decoupage
- Wire

- Beading
- Tatting
- Felting
- Weaving
- Stained glass
- Paper crafts
- Knife making
- Scale model building
- Embroidery
- Basket making

# #145 – Game clubs

Chess clubs are very popular and the library is a good place to facilitate a regular meeting. Also popular are cribbage, bridge, and role playing games. Unlike the Family game night (Program #165), where several games will be offered, get specific with this program by dedicating and embracing the patrons who love to play the chosen game.

**Target Audience:** Anyone interested

**Things needed:**
- A Facilitator – someone to lead the group (see How/Notes)
- The chosen game and plenty of it to accommodate the group
- A set of guidelines (or standard rules)
- A dedicated space to play

**Prep Time:** Minimal to arrange space

**Program Time:** 1 ½ - 2 hours

**Number of Participants:** Keep the group manageable. Less than 15, unless the library has a meeting room that can accommodate a larger group.

**Number of Friends/Volunteers needed:** The Facilitator should be able to handle the program.

**How/Notes:** Use an Interest Survey prior to setting up a game club. It isn't worth setting it up if there isn't interest, or possibly duplicates a club already in place somewhere else. For example, if the school has a thriving Chess Club, but several adults express interest, then consider adding Chess Club to the library's program list.

Recommend a Facilitator be assigned from within the group to:

- Communicate with the group and library staff
- Set-up tournaments, if desired
- Arbitrate any disputes with the game or conduct
- Provide instruction to new comers or as a library program

---

INTEREST SURVEY

We are trying to determine interest in some weekly or monthly gaming groups for the library. Please indicate by checkmark and circling any of the activities you'd be interested in attending.

- ☐ Card games (cribbage, bridge, canasta, Uno)
- ☐ Board games (chess, backgammon, Scrabble)
- ☐ Role playing games (Traveller, Savage Worlds, Dungeons & Dragons)
- ☐ Family Board games (Monopoly, Life, Clue, Sorry, Chinese checkers)
- ☐ Other – Please specify:_____

Thank you for your help! If you'd like to provide your name and contact information, we'll keep you posted.

Name _____ Age_____

Phone or email address _____

---

# #146 – Meatless Monday

Meatless Monday is a healthy eating movement with the intent of achieving a few things. By choosing a meatless option once a week, folks can see that vegetarian eating can be delicious and satisfying. There are political reasons, and the program can be designed to address the political side, but would be much more enjoyable to just focus on presenting some great recipes.

**Target Audience:** Everyone

**Things needed:**
- A Facilitator
- A few samples for tasting
- Recipe cards (optional but encouraged)

**Prep Time:** Minimal to arrange space

**Program Time:** An hour

**Number of Participants:** Limited only by space and fire code

**Number of Friends/Volunteers needed:** 1

**How/Notes:** Consider introducing protein options that may be new, or discussing the various consistencies of tofu and how to cook with each of them.
Also include:
- A nutrition discussion
- Maybe a game – Protein or not?
- Health benefits of various proteins (include meats to show the full spectrum)
- Maybe a list of restaurants in the area with great vegetarian menus?
- Infusing flavor into dishes

# #147 – Feng shui

Feng shui is an ancient Chinese philosophy that centers on all things having energy. It is, in essence, the study of environmental balance; a system that studies people's relationships with their environment, home and workspace, in order to achieve maximum harmony with the spiritual forces believed to influence all places. This program aims to facilitate those who are interested in learning more.

**Target Audience:** Anyone interested

**Things needed:**
- An Instructor/Facilitator
- Audiovisual support (utilize a slide presentation format with pictures to facilitate the information)
- The library's resources on the topic
- Samples

**Prep Time:** Minimal to arrange space

**Program Time:** An hour – utilize the half and half method. ½ hour of presentation, ½ hour of discussion and questions.

**Number of Participants:** Limited only by space and fire code, though a smaller group is recommended.

**Number of Friends/Volunteers needed:** 1

**How/Notes:** Recommend this program be conducted as a several week, or once a month series. There are too many facets of feng shui to cover in one sitting. It is best to give/receive information in small doses that can be applied slowly, over time. Consequently, consider including a little "homework assignment" for those interested, at the end of each session. The homework should focus on defining what is desired, assessing the current elements of the environment and adjusting to bring feng shui into balance.
Consider including the following topics:

- The basics – what is it and how can I bring the concepts into my life?
- The Elements of feng shui – the interaction of Fire, Earth, Metal, Water and Wood
- Feng shui Bagua – using the baguas to focus energy into other aspects of life (relationships, health, career, creativity, family etc.)
- Colors
- Decorating
- Room by room energy distribution
- At the office
- Out in the world
- Clutter control

How about re-arranging the program space as a practical exercise? This exercise won't work if the program is conducted in the stacks, however, it could be done on paper.

# #148 – Desk-top publishing

There are many stellar desktop publishing programs out there. So many possibilities to create professional looking products. This program will give participants a chance to learn the ins and outs of producing quality published documents for themselves and friends. Present this program as 4-6 week series and tackle a different type of product design each week.

**Target Audience:** Anyone interested

**Things needed:**
- An Instructor/Presenter
- Audiovisual support
- Samples of the project of the week
- The library's resources on the topic

**Prep Time:** Minimal to arrange space

**Program Time:** An hour

**Number of Participants:** Limited only by the number of available computers

**Number of Friends/Volunteers needed:** 1 + the Instructor/Presenter

**How/Notes:** This program should be presented as guided instruction, so the Instructor/Presenter needs to be very patient and outline all expectations at the beginning.
Possible topics:
- Document set-up
- Style for the document and audience
- Font size and readability (refer back to the introduction section for Chapter 4 for information on designing products intended to be read by seniors)
- Color scheme

- Margins and size
- Newsletters
- Flyers
- Menus/Cookbooks
- Business cards/Brochures
- Coupons
- Invitations

*"To build up a library is to create a life. It's never just a random collection of books." - Carlos Maria Dominguez, The House of Paper*

# #149 – Library clean-up day

Even if the library is professionally cleaned, there are still "deep cleaning" tasks patrons can help accomplish. Do the shelves need to be pulled out and cleaned behind? Does the display bulletin board glass need to be cleaned inside? Are those old, tired, faded decorations past their prime? Pick a day, make a list, gather cleaning supplies and volunteers and knock it out. Put on some music and "freshen up" the space.

**Target Audience:** Everyone

**Things needed:**
- A Facilitator/Leader
- A list of tasks
- Volunteers
- Cleaning supplies (depends on task list)
- Music (optional)
- Water
- Refreshments (optional but recommended at the end of the work party)

**Prep Time:** Only to make a list and gather needed supplies

**Program Time:** 1-3 hours depending on the list and the number of volunteers

**Number of Participants:** Hopefully many

**Number of Friends/Volunteers needed:** At least one to serve as Facilitator/Leader and manage the chore list and assign tasks.

**How/Notes:** Timing – Many folks will automatically think spring, for spring cleaning. But, maybe winterization is the goal. Planting bulbs for spring and prepping walkways for winter. Or, perhaps the library has a birthday celebration or large fundraiser at another time of the year, in which case, getting "the scrub on" would work best at that time.

In any case, asking for help goes a long way in creating a sense of ownership and pride in the library.

*"What I love most about libraries is that the books can only be borrowed, but the knowledge and inspiration they contain are yours to keep." Anthony Breznican*

# #150 – Dealing with a childhood medical diagnosis

My child has what? Hearing any kind of diagnosis about your child is awful. Some diagnoses are devastating and some are manageable with the right information and a game plan. Host this program as a series to help parents better understand their situation and connect with others who may have gone through, or are going through something similar.

**Target Audience:** Those interested

**Things needed:**
- A Presenter/Instructor (look to the local medical professional community)
- Audiovisual support (if needed)
- The library's resources on the topic
- Graphic training cards or reference sheets (check with the county extension office)

**Prep Time:** Minimal to arrange space

**Program Time:** 1 to 1½ hours. Utilize the half and half format (half the time on presentation of information and half the time dedicated to questions and discussion)

**Number of Participants:** Limited only by space and fire code

**Number of Friends/Volunteers needed:** 1 + Presenter/Instructor

**How/Notes:** A separate meeting room is preferred for this program to support the privacy of participants so they may freely discuss the issue.

Consider this as a series, or conducting an interest survey. Possible options include but are not limited to:
- Autism

- ADD/ADHD
- Behavior Disorders
- Eating Disorders
- Oppositional Defiant Disorder
- Obsessive Compulsive Disorder
- Anxiety Disorder
- Phobias

*"When life seems not worth living, ten minutes in a library proves otherwise."— Miv Schaaf*

# #151 – Author presentations & readings

Many communities are lucky enough to have a local author living there. If an author is available to come and read their work, what a boost for them and the library!

**Target Audience:** Everyone or just those interested (depends on the author and the work)

**Things needed:**
- Author
- Listeners
- Any audiovisual support requested by the Author
- Refreshments (optional)

**Prep Time:** About ½ hour to set out refreshments if offering, arrange space and set up audiovisual support if needed.

**Program Time:** 45 minutes to an hour

**Number of Participants:** Limited only by space and fire code

**Number of Friends/Volunteers needed:** 1 to introduce the Author

**How/Notes:** Remember! Although the library is typically prohibited from promoting individual work, "Story time" is fine. The Author can leave business cards or flyers for participants directing them to where their work is for sale.

If the Author wrote for children, adjust advertising and the time of the program. The other rules still apply.

Create a promotional display prior to the event.

# #152 – Couponing

Somewhere between paying full price, and couponing so extreme stores pay you, is couponing for the masses. Discuss tips and tricks for finding great deals and patrons will ask for this program over and over. It will be more popular than double-coupon Wednesdays!

**Target Audience:** Anyone interested

**Things needed:**
- A Facilitator/Instructor – someone well-versed in finding deals. Ask for a patron volunteer, or ask for an insider's perspective from a grocery store owner or manager.
- Audiovisual support (if needed)
- A list of on-line resources as a hand-out (optional)

**Prep Time:** Minimal to arrange space

**Program Time:** 1 hour

**Number of Participants:** Limited only by space and fire code

**Number of Friends/Volunteers needed:** 1

**How/Notes:** There are a lot of pitfalls to couponing websites and not understanding store policies. Make sure the discussion covers the cautionary tales.

# #153 – Flower arranging

Flower arranging is definitely an art form. Flowers are beautiful alone, but when artfully arranged, become something exceptional. There are a few basic "rules" of flower arranging and inviting a florist in for a demo and to field questions, would be fun.

**Target Audience:** Anyone interested

**Things needed:**
- An Instructor/Demonstrator – look to a local florist or nursery for a volunteer
- Sample vases
- Fillings
- Scissors
- Florist tape
- Flowers and greenery
- Instruction sheets

**Prep Time:** ½ hour to lay out supplies and arrange space

**Program Time:** 1 hour

**Number of Participants:** Instructor preference on how many they are comfortable accommodating.

**Number of Friends/Volunteers needed:** 1 to assist the Instructor/Demonstrator

**How/Notes:** Consider use of an overhead mirror if there is one available. Mirrors aid in showing participants close-up items without everyone having to gather around so closely.

Although it may be a little expensive, this program would really be terrific if participants could make an arrangement to take home.

# #154 – Night before school (back-to-school) dinner

Twas the night before school and all through the town, all the children's faces were stuck, in a permanent frown. The backpacks were hung by the door with great care, yet they still hoped that the bus driver would NOT be there. "I don't want to go yet!" they say with a whine. Hey! How about the library for a fun time?

Host a night before school dinner to shake off the jitters and get everyone jazzed up for heading back to school.

**Target Audience:** School aged children and their families

**Things needed:**
- Dinner makings – Recommend either a potluck or sandwich making fixings or a combination of both.
- Supplies for chosen activities (see How/Notes for ideas)

**Prep Time:** Will depend on how elaborate the party and activities chosen

**Program Time:** 2 hours (recommend 4:30 – 6:30 to make sure the kiddies get home and settled down)

**Number of Participants:** Limited by space, fire code and supplies

**Number of Friends/Volunteers needed:** Several depending on activities

**How/Notes:** Besides eating, play a few games. Recommended activities:
- Map pin – Have families put pins on a map of the country, indicating where they went this summer.
- Hope for the school year – Have a station where kids can write a goal for the school year
  - "I'd like to learn to count to 100."

- o "I want to read 20 books."
  - o "I want to improve my science grade over last year."
  - o "I plan on completing 10 scholarship applications."
- Hair braiding – My daughter likes to braid her hair at night and take it out in the morning so that it looks wavy. To do this, you'll need disposable combs (give it to the child to take) and a package of hair bands.
- Tutor connection sign-ups – start a board of possible tutors.
- Pin the tail on the teacher – an opportunity to "stick it to the teacher" so to speak.
- Get ready for school races. Stage a backpack, books, lunch pail, big coat and big galoshes along a route and have participants race to put it all together and get across the finish line.
- Give away fun pencils, or logo'd pencils from the Friends of the Library.
- Summer photo frame – lay out supplies to make a photo frame for a favorite summer memory.
- Backpack buddy – Lay out supplies to make a little doo-dad to hang on the backpack. Could be beaded, clay, feather or Shrinky Dinks®
- Healthy lunch choices game. Pack a pretend lunch with pictures of healthy and less healthy options.

# #155 – Digital scrapbooking

Scrapbooking is an artful presentation of preserved memories in a family album format. There are kits, conventions & whole sections of craft stores dedicated to this pastime. While beautiful in the finished piece, the equipment and supplies needed are expensive and take up a lot of space. An alternative – digital scrapbooking. The finished product is not the same, but all that is needed is a computer, the software (which most companies offer for free), the digital pictures that are already trapped on the computer, and time. Once done, the information is uploaded to the company providing the software, then bound into a keep-sake book. The cost may seem high, but when compared to traditional scrapbooking products, it isn't. This program is designed to introduce the concept of digital scrapbooking, demonstrate some work and answer questions.

**Target Audience:** Anyone interested

**Things needed:**
- An Instructor/Facilitator
- A computer
- A projector & screen
- Some "works in progress" to show and/or some finished books

**Prep Time:** About ½ hour to connect the audiovisual equipment, load projects and arrange space.

**Program Time:** An hour

**Number of Participants:** Limited only by space and fire code

**Number of Friends/Volunteers needed:** 1 (the Instructor/Facilitator can handle)

**How/Notes:** Consider some follow-on classes too. How about a series?

- Introduction
- Work on your own with some in-depth features
- Editing the work
- Creating backgrounds
- Journaling for successful scrapbooking

Some handy websites:
*http://www.picaboo.com*
*http://www.shutterfly.com*

# #156 – "Un"handyman class

Save some cash? Impress the ladies? Have an excuse to buy tools? Sponsor a program for the "un" handyman to gain some new skills and it won't matter why they come. This program aims to give some basic safety and project guidelines to take some of the fear out of potential do-it-yourselfers. There are so many potential topics, this program is recommended as a series.

**Target Audience:** Anyone interested

**Things needed:**
- A knowledgeable Presenter/Instructor – look to the local hardware store, general contractors, local business owners for support
- Audiovisual support (if needed)
- The library's resources on the topic
- Reference sheets (optional)
- Project sheets to take home (optional)

**Prep Time:** Minimal to arrange space

**Program Time:** 1 hour

**Number of Participants:** Limited only by space and fire code

**Number of Friends/Volunteers needed:** 1

**How/Notes:** The Presenter/Instructor needs to emphasize safety. My sister works in a hospital and sees a lot of people who thought they knew what they were doing, but chose to take safety shortcuts. Potential topics:
- The basic arsenal of needed equipment - Adhesives, tools (drill & drill bits, screwdriver set, wrench set, hammer), equipment (flashlights, extension cords, step ladder, tape measure, utility knife, level), safety equipment (gloves, glasses, fire extinguisher)

- The slow build – before tackling a big project, what are some smaller projects that can be done? Or, incorporate the buddy system and help a friend.
- Planning – ever heard the phrase "Measure twice, cut once?" A good plan and precise measurements will save a project from disaster.
- Timing – how long should a job take? And, drying time is not something to avoid or shortcut.
- Setting up a workspace
- Reference material and resources (hey, how about checking out the library?)
- Gasket or grommet? How do I identify all of this stuff?
- How to fix a running toilet
- Repairing drywall
- Fix sticky drawers
- Safety! – Ladders, electrical, turning off sources BEFORE starting a project
- Patch a gutter leak
- How to do common electrical repairs
- Troubleshooting

# #157 – Conversational English (ESL)

Welcoming non-English speaking patrons into the library will return in spades.

**Target Audience:** Non-English speaking patrons

**Things needed:**
- An Instructor/Facilitator
- Audiovisual support (if needed)
- English speaking volunteers to help
- A list of topics to talk about
- Conversion dictionary so that each participant can look things up as needed
- Refreshments (optional)

**Prep Time:** Minimal to arrange space and set up audiovisual support

**Program Time:** An hour

**Number of Participants:** Registration is recommended on this program to ensure that there are enough English speakers to support the conversation.

**Number of Friends/Volunteers needed:** Will depend on registration numbers and if offering refreshments

**How/Notes:** This program could be a reciprocal program where one week English is spoken and the next week, another language is addressed.

Utilize this program as a reciprocal program to the Conversational language series (Program #104).

# #158 – Home brewing basics

Many people are interested in exploring the process of creating artisan quality beers at home. Home brewing has grown in popularity to the "we have our own conventions" numbers. This program will explore the good, the bad, and the tried and true. Participants will be able to ask questions and hopefully avoid some of the pitfalls of learning a new craft.

**Target Audience:** Those interested

**Things needed:**
- An Instructor/Facilitator
- Samples (if allowed)
- Audiovisual support (if needed)
- The library's resources on the topic
- An additional resource list (optional)

**Prep Time:** Minimal to arrange space

**Program Time:** An hour

**Number of Participants:** Limited only by Instructor/Facilitator preference and space available. If offering samples, registration and age verification will be needed.

**Number of Friends/Volunteers needed:** 1-2

**How/Notes:** Ensure discussion includes ingredients, equipment and processes, as well as, space and ventilation requirements.

# #159 – Community weight loss challenge

Trying to lose weight can be challenging and exasperating. But with the support of others and fun activities to look forward to, all of a sudden, it becomes less burdensome and much more enjoyable. Even if the results are slow, the camaraderie of doing something together and lifting each other up is a satisfying reward. Start a 3 month long community weight loss challenge and incorporate a combination of group meetings, recipe tips and exercise activities.

**Target Audience:** Anyone interested

**Things needed:**
- A Facilitator to organize activities and track progress
- A big scale (like the weigh station on the highway if there is one nearby, or at any shipping company)
- A plan (see How/Notes for ideas)
- Supplies to support the plan

**Prep Time:** Getting the word out is the most difficult piece of this program. Recommend going to the local radio station, social media and newspaper for this one. Otherwise, prep work is minimal.

**Program Time:** 3 months with varying times for events along the way.

**Number of Participants:** As many as possible

**Number of Friends/Volunteers needed:** Depends on the programs chosen

**How/Notes:** Some people are motivated by reward. In this plan, the only reward offered is a sense of community support and individual accomplishment. If incentives are offered, then consider weighing and measuring participants individually instead of as a group.
It is natural to assume that I would recommend January to start this program, but there are so many gyms and health clubs offering

incentives in January, it would be rude to compete with them. Instead, partner with them and consider March – May. Initial New Year's resolution enthusiasm has waned, the weather is improving in most of the country and swimsuit season is just around the corner.

Ideas for events:
- Weekly walk/ride – Meet at the library on Saturday morning and take off. Plan a 30 minute trek and an hour long trek so that participants have options. * A fun add on – keep track of the miles covered by each group, and at the end, calculate how far they traveled on a map.
- Evening yoga (which standard 9-5ers would enjoy), or yoga in the morning on the lawn if available.
- Zumba (open early or open after hours to support Zumba or other aerobics class)
- Calisthenics stations – put on fun music and every two minutes move to a new station and conduct the exercise (jumping jacks, sit ups, pushups etc.)
- Cut the fat recipe over-haul weekly, or the meatless Monday program (#146), or chef demonstrations (Program #114)
- Weekly talk & support. Make it at a time of day to capture as many participants as possible, perhaps before or right after the Saturday morning event.
- Motivation board – little reminder cards. At the beginning, have participants write cards to motivate themselves. Why are you doing this? What do you hope to gain? Who is your inspiration? Post the cards where participants can regularly see them.
- Social media – post tips and motivational tidbits.

# #160 – Wedding or party planning

The elements of throwing a great party all boil down to the same thing whether it is an elaborate wedding, a kid's birthday party or a Super Bowl bash with friends.... planning. This program is designed to help participants consider the coordination and timeline needed to make all of their events special.

**Target Audience:** Anyone interested

**Things needed:**
- An Instructor/Facilitator
- Audiovisual support (if needed)
- A planning matrix for participants to take with them (many options available online)
- Table and decorations to work with
- Refreshments (optional, but recommended. Use easy to prepare but impactful party food)

**Prep Time:** About ½ hour to arrange the space

**Program Time:** 1 ½ - 2 hours (if setting up a tablescape)

**Number of Participants:** Registration recommended to keep things manageable

**Number of Friends/Volunteers needed:** 1 + Instructor/Facilitator

**How/Notes:** This could easily be a 3-4 part series, which would cut down on the program time. Discuss the following:
- Deciding on a theme
- Timeline (when should invitations go out? Things to do in the weeks before and days before)
- Venues (conventional and unexpected)
- Decorations
- Food & Beverage planning
- Delegating responsibilities

- Being the 'hostess with the mostest' - how to have fun at your own party
- Tablescapes
- Displaying food
- Music
- Photographers
- Party favors
- Handling the "oops" moments

*"What in the world would we do without our libraries?" – Katharine Hepburn*

# #161 – Home schooling

Should I choose private school, public school, or home school for my child? Parents with the flexibility to make these choices, struggle with choosing the right path for their child's education. Host a discussion-style program and present pros & cons.

**Target Audience:** Specialized – Parents of school aged children

**Things needed:**
- A Presenter/Facilitator (look for a volunteer either a current homeschooling family, or the school district homeschool coordinator)
- Audiovisual support (if needed)
- Website resource list (optional)

**Prep Time:** Minimal to arrange space

**Program Time:** An hour

**Number of Participants:** Limited only by space and fire code

**Number of Friends/Volunteers needed:** 1

**How/Notes:** Cover the following on readiness:
- The time commitment – homeschooling requires a lot of prep work as well as instructional work. Plus there are papers to grade, field trips, experiments, projects, coordination with the host school district etc.
- Personal dedication – it is important to remember to take care of yourself and have time alone – don't leave this out of the discussion.
- Household organization – a dedicated space for the school day (even if it transitions to a different space later) is essential. And, the chores may come second (or even third) sometimes.

- Whole family buy-in – the child and other adults in the house must also be on-board with homeschooling or it may not be successful.
- Finances – Homeschooling itself isn't too expensive, but the loss of the income of the parent who is teaching may put a strain on the family's finances.
- Technology requirements
- Socialization – It is important to get homeschooled children out to interact with other kids, but with homeschooling there is a benefit of being able to choose which kids your child spends time with, and when.
- One year at a time – it is important to note that homeschooling isn't a school-career commitment and most families make the decision year by year.
- Why did others make the leap? Solicit the stories of others.
- The intimidation of being "the teacher" – yes – it is hard, but there are some great curriculums out there. And, hey! You learned it once before, right?

# #162 – Home school connection

Home schoolers need to occasionally come to the library anyway. So, why not host a regular get together where families can meet, exchange ideas and/or engage in an educational presentation?

**Target Audience:** Home school children and their teachers

**Things needed:**
- A Facilitator/and sometimes a Presenter
- Audiovisual support (if needed)
- Library's resources on presentations (this will require coordination between the Presenter and the library staff)
- Snacks (optional)

**Prep Time:** ½ hour to arrange space and set up audiovisual equipment

**Program Time:** 1 – 1 ½ hours

**Number of Participants:** Limited only by space and fire code

**Number of Friends/Volunteers needed:** 1

**How/Notes:** Take a poll each time to get a feel for what is being studied throughout the group. Look for ways to "cross walk" ages and grades with over-arching presentations that will engage all students.

Perhaps offer map reading classes and activities, science exploration or language immersion – whatever is needed or desired from the group.

Keep a running list of ideas.

Consider asking in speakers and discussing requirements with school administrators to better support the home school community.

Recommend offering "get to know you" events too, so the children can connect socially with each other. At these events, provide "time and talents" surveys to find out where expertise lies. These surveys may even generate new Friends of the Library!

*"There wasn't a place I could think of that was more magical than a building bursting with books and stories and words..." - Lindsay Eland, <u>A Summer of Sundays</u>*

# #163 – Foreign exchange program information

Foreign exchange programs offer students and host families a unique look into the language and culture of a far-away land. Students study, while host families provide housing and insight into the culture from their perspective. Host a program at the library to discuss the in's and out's of various exchange programs.

**Target Audience:** Those interested

**Things needed:**
- A Presenter – look for volunteers who have been involved before, either as a student or host family
- Audiovisual support (if needed)

**Prep Time:** Minimal to arrange space

**Program Time:** An hour on the ½ and ½ format. ½ hour for presentation and ½ hour for questions and discussion.

**Number of Participants:** Limited only by space and fire code

**Number of Friends/Volunteers needed:** 1

**How/Notes:** Make sure families tune into:
- Why do they want to be involved in a foreign exchange program?
- What country or countries are of interest to participants?
- What are the student or host requirements?
- What are the costs (+ the hidden costs) and are there scholarship options?

For a complete list of available program, look at the webpage for the Council on Standards for International Educational Travel (CSIET) at *http://www.csiet.org*

# #164 – Family art

A family that creates together has a better sense of each other and will have a greater level of respect and regard for each other. My opinion, of course, but giving families a chance to do things together should be a key part of any Friends programming plan. This is a program I designed at my library and it was part of a family art series. Series or alone, the concept is this: The family works together to create one piece of frame-worthy art. This would also be fun to do as part of a marriage enrichment series. This program costs a bit for supplies, but is well worth it. The work itself is easy – the set-up and execution is a little tricky.

**Target Audience:** Families/couples

**Things needed:**
- 8 ½" x 11" or larger hardboard canvases
- Painters tape (if the piece is framed, the edges won't show. A pencil line or tape will define the viewable space. Or, use painters tape or marker to section out and each member paints a section if they want)
- A variety of mediums (acrylic paint, watercolor paint, watercolor pencils, oil pastels, charcoal pencil, markers)
- Paint brushes and water cups (lots of them)
- A bucket & pitcher (for dumping paint water into and refill water cups)
- Drop cloths (if needed)
- Drying space

**Prep Time:** ½ - 1 hour to set out supplies. Recommend separating mediums into different areas around the library or space.

**Program Time:** 1 ½ - 2hours + Story Time (Story Time works well as a drying time activity), or the book plate program (Program #128)

**Number of Participants:** As many as the venue can comfortably hold and can be budgeted for. Registration is required for this program and two time slots work well. If there is one time slot, the program will be limited to fewer participants, if there are two time slots, it is less likely that people will be on top of each other and more participants can be served.

**Number of Friends/Volunteers needed:** 2-3

**How/Notes:** There is no definition of what family means for this program. Since it is meant to be a 'come together' type project, there should be at least two participants per canvas.

When families check in, they are given their canvas and pointed in the direction of each station ("oil pastels over there, acrylic over there, markers there")

Families produce their masterpiece together and have loads of fun!

Participants either stay for Story Time while their project dries (Story Time should start at the 30 minute mark, or slightly later, from the program start time). Or, they can take their piece home as soon as they're done with it.

Recommend avoiding oil paint since small children will be involved, and it both resembles finger paint and stains a lot!

Recommend having slips of paper available for folks to write their names on to slide under their projects while drying.

# #165 – Family game night

Buy the games and they will come. That is the key to establishing and maintaining a great family game night. It is best for the Friends to purchase several quality games appealing to a wide range of ages, then take suggestions from patrons for more. Keep some of the games available at the library for use any time. This is a great once a month, drop-in style program. Once things are established, there will be 'regulars.' Start with a Friend facilitating, but it won't be long before a 'regular' takes over. Time to recruit him/her into the Friends!

**Target Audience:** Everyone

**Things needed:** Games, and flat spaces to play games

**Prep Time:** Just a few minutes to set out the games and arrange the space.

**Program Time:** Since it is drop-in style, a 1 ½ - 2 hour window works well.

**Number of Participants:** Varies depending on the space and the games provided

**Number of Friends/Volunteers needed:** Will depend on the number of participants. Recommend a ratio of 20:1

**How/Notes:** Lay out the games and have some fun!
Have participants decide amongst themselves the rule set they'll use prior to starting play.

Think about expanding and offering tournaments (Program #130)
Or, borrow games from a local toy store to see if people will like them. This is great free publicity for the store.

Offer tutorials on unfamiliar games like Pokemon card games, Magic, canasta, pinochle, dominoes – you name it.

*"A library is more than a brick and mortar building filled with delicious books. It is also a community of people who live to invest in our youth, who read for knowledge and fun, and who are ready to include anyone who walks through the door." Kate. L. McGarry*

# Chapter 6 – Get new patrons – Exposure ideas

With the internet, creative new apps, blogs, schools, sports teams, new stores opening, food preparation get-togethers and a plethora of other time grabbers – the more it seems we are communicating less with each other, it also seems as if we can't get away from information saturation. Sometimes it feels as if we are fracturing into smaller pockets within the community rather than looking for ways to come together as a community. This section presents a few simple ideas for getting people interested in coming into the library to see what's new.

First and foremost, put out a **Suggestion Box** – And mean it! Make sure when a suggestion is acted on, that everyone knows that it came from the Suggestion Box. And, make note of suggestions that were considered but didn't fit – why – and thank the person who made the suggestion, if possible.

# #166 – Guessing jar

Jelly Beans near Easter, red hot hearts or candy kisses for Valentine's Day, candy corn for Halloween. Whatever the occasion, a guessing jar is entertaining for everyone. The sneaky benefit of improving math estimating skills need not be mentioned to young participants who really just want to win the sweet treats. So much so that they may beg to come to the library <u>every</u> <u>day</u> to guess!

**Target Audience:** Ages 12 & under

**Things needed:**
- A jar or other clear container with a tight fitting lid
- Candy or other items which are worth winning, maybe marbles or jacks
- Slips of paper pre-printed with "Name, Age, Phone number, Guess" lines for guessing
- Container to hold guesses

**Prep Time:** One hour to purchase items and jar, count and display

**Program Time:** 1 ½ to 2 weeks

**Number of Participants:** Hopefully many

**Number of Friends/Volunteers needed:** 1

**How/Notes:** Make sure that the container stays closed when patrons pick it up.

Discount or other second-hand/consignment shops are great places to find interesting containers. Recommend clear plastic so that items can be seen and if the container is dropped, it is less likely to break. This program would be a nice addition to the Library Birthday Party (Program #180), Silent Auction (Program #189), the last few weeks of Summer Reading, or any other large event at the library.

Have a habitual winner? Consider a textured or fluted, oddly shaped container, or a decoy (this is something placed inside the container that displaces items inside to throw off the "counters."

*"If you want to find your happy place, just go to the library." Lizzie K. Foley, Author*

# #167 – "Best of" flyers

Coming in new to a community sparks a sense of awakening to new possibilities; but also sometimes imparts fear of the unknown. Where are the best places? What makes this place unique? No one wants to waste their money, so "Best of" flyers are helpful tidbits from those in-the-know. Look to include specialized hours of operation, unique accommodations, festivals, and other special events.

**Target Audience:** Everyone

**Things needed:**
- Surveys
- A place to put the flyers
- Eye-catching graphics

**Prep Time:** Surveys should run about a month, then a week or two to prep and print flyers.

**Program Time:** On-going/Annually

**Number of Participants:** N/A

**Number of Friends/Volunteers needed:** 1-3 – Recommend the Teen Council produce the flyers, possibly with the help of the high school graphics department or local designer.

**How/Notes:** Make sure that the flyers note that the library is in no way a sponsor of anyone highlighted in a "Best of" flyer. The information provided is based on votes by the community. Use an on-line survey provider or include printed copies in the annual newsletter, or utilize social media to take nominees.

Consider categories such as:
- Best fall colors drive
- Scariest haunted houses/best Easter egg hunts/most festive holiday light displays

- Best kite-flying locations
- Best local sandwich/pizza/soup etc. (make this specific down to the menu item)
- Most educational or entertaining museums
- Best late-night bites
- Best surfing spots
- Best cranberry recipes
- Best prom 'up-do' providers
- Best doggie day-care
- Best kid's menu
- Most vegetarian variety

The list could go on & on. Think about what is available in the community and what people might have a strong opinion about (Pat's vs. Gino's for cheese-steak in Philadelphia comes to mind). The on-going debate will spark people to vote and give press to the library for hosting.

# #168 – Show up tickets

People really like the idea of entering a drawing and winning a prize, especially if they know there won't be a sales call afterwards. No pressure here, just an opportunity to win something – for FREE. Run this program a couple of times a year. The end result will be an increase in traffic and circulation, which will make the library the WINNER!

**Target Audience:** Everyone

**Things needed:**
- Tickets – Either homemade or purchased (Just need to have room for a phone number and name)
- Prizes – Friends merchandise or credit at the book sale are good choices
- A container for entries
- A placard announcing the winner (optional)

**Prep Time:** Minimal – only to make tickets and advertise

**Program Time:** On-going for a week or two

**Number of Participants:** Everyone

**Number of Friends/Volunteers needed:** 1

**How/Notes:** Look at last year's circulation and traffic numbers and choose the lowest month to try the event. Make sure to note the increase in traffic from the event in the annual newsletter.
Solicit donations from local businesses, perhaps once a quarter or so.

# #169 – Library card drive

Who is eligible for a library card? What are the benefits of having a library card? Put together a goal and a small media blitz and have fun gathering new patrons.

**Target Audience:** Non-library patrons

**Things needed:**
- A flyer of services and library card rules, with detachable library card registration form.
- A goal and plan
- A mobile location (optional)
- Registration gifts (optional – consider a coupon for book sale credit or a punch card for extended check out on movies etc.)
- Dynamic volunteers

**Prep Time:** Prep is dedicated to formulating the plan and getting the word out.

**Program Time:** Depends. Could be a monthly thing, or an on-going push, or run for a month at the end of the school year. Format will need to be library-dependent.

**Number of Participants:** Hopefully many

**Number of Friends/Volunteers needed:** 2-3, possibly more depending on format

**How/Notes:** The key to this program is finding out where the underserved population is in the community and seeking to target them.

Consider a partnership with the local school(s), craft fairs, the county fair, community festivals, and theatre events. Really, anywhere folks gather is worth a booth or table. Make a tracking board with the goal on it, so everyone can see progress.

A realistic goal is an annual increase of 5% higher than the normal rate of growth.

*"The library is like a candy store where everything is free." – Jamie Ford, <u>Songs of Willow Frost</u>*

# #170 – Welcome basket

Some communities offer a welcome basket to new-comers through the Chamber of Commerce or City Hall. If that is the case, drop a piece of logo'd merchandise with a card or magnet that has the library's hours listed. Also include a copy of last year's annual newsletter. This will show the new residents that the library is a welcoming and active place.

**Target Audience:** New residents

**Things needed:**
- A piece of logo'd Friends of the Library merchandise (recommend something that will fit everyone like a cup, mouse pad, book bag or mug)
- A card or magnet with the library's hours
- Annual newsletter

**Prep Time:** Only time to run the items over to the Chamber of Commerce or City Hall

**Program Time:** On-going

**Number of Participants:** N/A

**Number of Friends/Volunteers needed:** 1 to keep up the stock and keep track of items donated

**How/Notes:** Make sure the Treasurer keeps track of the donated items, at cost, in the loss column on the Treasurer's report.

If there isn't a welcome program in the city, the library can still do one. The 'basket' can be a bag or mug with items placed inside. Or maybe a pencil bouquet? If the program is run through the library, recommend it be limited to new adult library card applicants. Do something for the young new library card applicants too, just on a smaller, less expensive scale.

# #171 – Adopt a sister library

According to the American Library Association flyer, *The Sister Library Program*, a quote from Sarah Ann Long says "becoming a Sister Library is an opportunity to build relationships with libraries in other cultures that can help us learn, understand and better serve our own community." The American Library Association encourages U.S. libraries to form relationships with libraries in other countries. The idea is to improve access to materials in both countries, raise awareness of issues and needs facing libraries, and share technologies and techniques.

**Target Audience:** Anyone interested

**How/Notes:** Things that can be done with the Sister Library:
- Organize pen pal programs
- Organize a delegation of patrons and staff to visit the Sister Library
- Exchange newsletters, local newspapers, cultural materials, photos and program ideas
- Assist in procurement of materials

# #172 – Rotating display

A display case used to display patron treasures does a few things: It develops a sense of ownership in the library, creates a focal point of interest, connects people with similar interests and inspires others to develop their own unique collections/art pieces.

**Target Audience:** Everyone

**Things needed:**
- Either a stand-alone, wall-mounted or wall inset display case
- A set of guidelines for patron displays
- A release of liability form
- A list of who is scheduled. Recommend reserving up to 8 or 9 months in advance. Also, ask folks when they sign up if they would be available sooner if needed, or if there are months they'll be unavailable (snow birds, Summer camp)

**Prep Time:** Give the patron next on the list a call at least a week ahead of time.

**Program Time:** Patron displays should rotate on a monthly basis.

**Number of Participants:** 1 per month

**Number of Friends/Volunteers needed:** 1 to manage the list and notifications

**How/Notes:** The initial cost for a quality display case will range from expensive to very expensive. Deals or a donation may be available, but look to compliment the décor and feel of the library.

# #173 – Give-aways

As a Friends group, the mission may be to promote reading in the community, but it may also be to increase library patronage. One way of doing this is to appeal to the younger crowd. If they know there is a special "treat" waiting for them when they get to the library, it may motivate them to want to come more often. Plus, give aways are fun for everyone! This is a relatively passive program with a big pay-off.

**Target Audience:** Everyone

**Things needed:**
- Pencils (Seasonal or with the library's name and phone number)
- Pens
- Magnets with the library's information printed on them
- Coupons for Book Sale credit (valid on the next visit)
- Tattoos (think seasonal, Halloween, Valentine's Day etc.)
- Stickers
- Hand stamps
- Bookmarks

**Prep Time:** Only to purchase & decide what the give-away of the day or week will be.

**Program Time:** On-going

**Number of Participants:** Anyone interested

**Number of Friends/Volunteers needed:** 1 to manage purchases

**How/Notes:** The library staff will know what patrons get excited about, so make sure they are consulted.

If buying on-line, purchase enough product with enough seasonal variety that the order qualifies for free shipping. The stuff will keep and reduces the number of times items will need to be ordered and tracked.

A note about bookmarks – bookmarks are often sent by publishers and provided for free. However, consider compiling scrap paper, stickers and other notions, and hosting a bookmark making day (not a program listed, just a bonus thought) Display these bookmarks as handmade by patrons and free with a donation encouraged, or sell them at the photography and art show fundraiser (Program #192).

This would be a good Teen Council project.

# #174 – Visiting art display

If the library is lucky enough to have a university, high school or local art gallery nearby, extend the invitation to host some of the art. A program like this creates wonderful symbiotic relationships. Introduction to art up-close for young people, exposure for a local artist, advertisement for the university, school or gallery, and variety for the library.

**Target Audience:** Everyone

**Things needed:**
- Coordinator/Facilitator
- Space – this program will require a dedicated space to host the visiting art.
- An agreement between the art owner and the library
- Liability insurance to cover the visiting art (possibly) or a release from liability
- Placards and descriptions
- The library's resources on the style and medium presented (optional, but recommended near the art display)

**Prep Time:** Only set-up and coordination time is required

**Program Time:** On-going

**Number of Participants:** N/A

**Number of Friends/Volunteers needed:** The Coordinator/Facilitator to assist with set-up and production of placards and descriptions.

**How/Notes:** Consider incorporating a visiting art display into other programs such as the art series (Program #82), Wine and cheese tasting (Program #85)

# #175 – Spring seed and fall bulb exchange

My neighbor came by recently and asked if I would like to have some of her yellow lilies in exchange for my variegated red/orange ones. Well, yes I would, what a great idea! And, furthermore, what a great idea for a fun library get-together. Bring out the library's resources on gardening for a great kick-start to planting season.

**Target Audience:** Anyone interested

**Things needed:**
- A Coordinator/Facilitator
- Paper
- Markers
- Tape
- Bags – Paper for bulbs, smaller snack sized zip-style for smaller seeds
- Refreshments (optional)

**Prep Time:** About an hour to set up tables and arrange space

**Program Time:** 1 – 1 ½ hours

**Number of Participants:** Limited only by space and fire code

**Number of Friends/Volunteers needed:** 2 – 3 depending on # of participants, including the Coordinator/Facilitator

**How/Notes:** Make sure advertising specifies that this is a free event and bringing seeds to share is not necessary, but is encouraged. The more volume and variety of seeds the better.

Recommend pre-arranging at least a half dozen or so volunteer "traders."

Partner with the local garden club, or ask patrons for potential seed givers. When arranging space, provide space for the known participants, plus allow extra space for those who bring seeds to set up too.

Ask traders to attractively display their items on trays, or in bowls etc.

Encourage non-hybridized seeds, as they are most likely to be productive. Some hybrid seeds are sterile, while others are unpredictable.

Also, include a talk on how to harvest and save seeds. Address:
- Which plants thrive from seed
- Heirloom varieties of regional plants
- The differences between non-hybridized and hybrid seeds

Try these websites for more help:
*http://www.heirloomseedswap.com* and
*http://www.southernexposure.com*

# #176 – Welcome baby donation

The purpose of this idea is to reach potential new patrons. If the mission of the Friends is "to promote reading in the community," then this program hits the mark. Many hospitals provide new parent baskets with products and services they'll need. Get on board and show parents the value of the library in their new baby's life.

**Target Audience:** New parents and their babies

**Things needed:**
- Beautifully bound baby board books
- Book plate indicating that the book is provided by the Friends of the Library

**Prep Time:** Prep time will be dedicated to making the connection at the hospital, purchasing the books and applying the book plates.

**Program Time:** On-going

**Number of Participants:** N/A

**Number of Friends/Volunteers needed:** 1 to manage purchasing and distribution.

**How/Notes:** Connect with the local hospital to get a feel for the yearly average for budgeting purposes. If the numbers are large, consider requesting donations or having a special fundraiser. Possible fundraiser titles:
- Books for Babies
- Oh, baby! Book sale
- Old books for new babies

# #177 – Annual newsletter

Pat yourselves on the back! As a Friends group, you've worked hard all year to provide quality programming and raise money for the library. Sum it all up into an annual newsletter along with an application to join the Friends and watch what happens. Psst. It will be new Friends of the Library!

**Target Audience:** Everyone

**Things needed:**
- A Coordinator/Record-keeper
- Data
- Format (trifold mailer? Full sheet?)
- Distribution method (mass mailing, email, website, or Chamber of Commerce website? Or a combination approach?)

**Prep Time:** Good record keeping will help pull the data together quickly. Prep time is dedicated to writing and editing; then printing and preparing chosen distribution method(s).

**Program Time:** Once annually

**Number of Participants:** N/A

**Number of Friends/Volunteers needed:** Several

**How/Notes:** Data to include:
- Vision and Mission statements
- Goals for next year
- A list of programs conducted and number of people who attended each
- Traffic numbers this year vs. last year
- Circulation numbers this year vs. last year
- Amount of money spent on programming
- Amount of money raised/donated

- A list of major donors with another Thank You
- Amount of money spent on supplies and/or equipment for the library
- Survey of desired programs (include programs that are being considered already)
- Application for Friends membership
- Calendar of regularly scheduled programs (coffee chat, story time, writing groups, book clubs, game groups)

*"There is more treasure in books than in all the pirate's loot on Treasure Island." Walt Disney*

# #178 – Drop-in activities

Drop-in activities are commonly referred to as passive programs, meaning that they are fairly simple to do and garner interest in the coming to the library. And, isn't that the goal of this whole book? Any time folks are looking for something to do and the library is open, the goal is to get them to think about the library as an option. Having a few fun drop-in activities is a good way to plant the seed.

**Target Audience:** Everyone

**Things needed:**
- Drop-in activities and a way to get the information out to patrons

**Prep Time:** Very little

**Program Time:** On-going

**Number of Participants:** Hopefully many

**Number of Friends/Volunteers needed:** 1 to monitor and replenish supply levels

**How/Notes:** How about the following as a start?
- A selection of board games and brain teasers
- An on-going community story (people drop-in and vote for the next line and write suggestions for the line after that, or plot twist ideas, characters, locations etc.)
- Coloring sheets
- Daily Mad Lib (each person who comes in gets to fill-in the next blank, then post the finished piece on social media – fun to do once a week)
- Reader's theatre scripts (fun for groups to do)
- Puppets
- A daily or weekly movie with coloring sheets

- Guess the book – post a line from a book and the first person to get it right wins a small prize or a small amount in book sale credit.
- Mystery match – a color of the day wins a special prize
- Trivia questions to earn credit at the Book Sale

*"All you need in life is truth and beauty and you can find both at the Public Library." Studs Terkel*

# #179 – Local parade participation

Sing it with me... I love a parade! What a way to showcase the library to the community. Cut loose and have some fun!

**Target Audience:** Everyone

**Things needed:**
- Give aways – Check the rules. Some towns require parade entrants to hand out their give aways, while others allow things to be tossed to parade goers. Recommend pencils, magnets or bookmarks with the library hours, or "read" tattoos
- Something to carry the give aways in – consider the parade theme
- Volunteers – the more the merrier
- A theme
- A banner
- Good weather
- Music (optional)

**Prep Time:** Will depend on how extensive the participation. A float will require much more work and effort than a banner and a few people in costume.

**Program Time:** Length of the parade plus line-up time

**Number of Participants:** All parade goers

**Number of Friends/Volunteers needed:** Several

**How/Notes:** Depending on interest – consider a Book Cart Drill Team. The entertainment value is nearly on par with the Shriners and their little cars (ok, maybe not THAT cool, but close). Add some fabulous music and hear the fans scream "I want to go to the LIBRARY!"

# #180 – Throw a library birthday party

Hey, another song! Celebrate good times, c'mon! Put out some cake, punch and let the good times roll.

**Target Audience:** Everyone

**Things needed:**
- Birthday party decorations
- Cake & punch with plates, forks, napkins and cups
- Tablecloths and extra garbage cans and liners
- Activities – Supply needs will depend on activities chosen
- Music (optional, but recommended)

**Prep Time:** A few hours to arrange space and lay out supplies

**Program Time:** Run time will depend on the size of the library. A large branch with lots of activities should plan on about 4 hours. A small branch with a small patron base could go with 3 hours.

**Number of Participants:** Limited only by space and fire code

**Number of Friends/Volunteers needed:** Several – will depend on activities chosen

**How/Notes:** Get a large cake. Running out of cake is awful! So says the lover of cake.
Consider the following activities:
- Face painting – A birthday party classic that never fails to draw a crowd
- A magician – look for a patron who wants the practice and will do it for free
- Balloon animals
- Story telling
- Limbo
- Paint bookends (Program #119)
- Make book plates (Program #128)

- Skills demonstrations (Program #134)
- Library services tour including a look "behind the scenes" (Program #121)

*"Libraries offer, for free, the wisdom of the ages - and sages - and, simply put, there's something for everyone inside." Laura Bush*

# #181 – Delivery service

Bookmobiles are wonderful! But, the high cost of upkeep, maintenance and staffing have caused many library systems to drop the beloved bookmobile from the list of services offered.
Free or fee, whatever the choice, an outreach of delivery service shows patrons that the whole community is important to the library.

**Target Audience:** Specialized – home bound individuals, shift workers like nurses & firefighters

**Things needed:**
- A Coordinator
- A plan or charter
- Deliverers (volunteers)
- Delivery method (bikes/vehicles)
- Something to carry materials back and forth in – specially marked messenger bags perhaps?
- Receipt method

**Prep Time:** The majority of prep time will go into the plan

**Program Time:** On-going

**Number of Participants:** Limited to delivery area

**Number of Friends/Volunteers needed:** Will depend on the availability of services offered and popularity of the program. But, volunteers will be the glue of this program. Without dedicated volunteers, don't even attempt this endeavor.

**How/Notes:** This would make an interesting senior class or Eagle Scout project. Take "orders" somehow and swap current materials for new. I'd love to see bicycles delivering library materials.

While developing the plan, take into consideration:
- Delivery area – what kind of distance radius is sustainable?

- Who will do the deliveries and when? Senior class students may not be able to deliver during the school day, but the coffee chat seniors could.
- How often will deliveries be offered?
- What kind of liability insurance will be required, if any?
- How will the program be advertised?
- Will the program be free or fee?
- What to do if items can't be delivered to a person?

# #182 – Host a volkssporting event

Volkssporting started in Germany and is defined as a personal fitness sports and recreation program offering noncompetitive sporting events like walks, hikes, bike rides, swims and sometimes cross-country skiing. Participants choose their start time within a start/finish window and participate at their own pace.

Volkssporting is supported in the United States by the American Volkssport Association (AVA). They have local chapters all over the country and have all of the information needed to set up a volksmarch (walking event) or other volkssporting event at any location, including a library. The benefits of connecting with the AVA to put together an event will draw new patrons to the library, and should be of no cost to the library (free publicity). Many people associated with the AVA travel to places specifically for events or unique walks.

An event can be a one-time occurrence, or an on-going event where the materials are stored in the library and people who want to do the event can come, pay the fee and sign themselves in.

**Target Audience:** Everyone

**Things needed:**
- A Coordinator – someone who will work with the local chapter to put the event together
- Event sanctioning – this is required by the AVA
- Tables (for a one-time event)
- Water and snacks (for a one-time event)
- A place to put the materials (everything needed fits easily into a suitcase style file box) (for an on-going event)
- Trained library staff (for an on-going event). It is essential that the library staff be aware of what the box is and where it is located when someone asks for it.

**Prep Time:** Time to coordinate with the local AVA Chapter and set up the event, write the map etc.

**Program Time:** Will depend on the event chosen

**Number of Participants:** Limitless

**Number of Friends/Volunteers needed:** Will depend on the size and extent of the event. If the event is on-going, someone from the local AVA chapter will be assigned to tend to the box and no additional library support will be required.

**How/Notes:** All events, whether they are on-going or one-time events must be sanctioned by the AVA. The process isn't difficult, but a partnership with a local chapter is the only way to make it happen. So, get with the local chapter, design a walk or sponsor an event, or make the walk part of the Community weight loss challenge (Program #159), Healthy, wealthy, nifty and thrifty series (Program #76), Turn off the TV week activities (Program #140), or as a pre-cursor to a fund-raising event like the Band Jam (Program #188), Sidewalk chalk art contest (Program #187), Book sale (Program #195).

# #183 – New material features

An interesting display of new materials should be something to look forward to each and every time the library is visited. Work to make it extra special and it will be adored, admired and savored by all. This idea aims to take displaying new materials to the next level. As Emeril Legasse says, "let's kick it up a notch."

**Target Audience:** Everyone

**Things needed:**
- A Coordinator
- Imagination
- Dedicated space
- Social media

**Prep Time:** Once done, it is a matter of upkeep. Prep time will depend on what is already in place and how extensive the plan.

**Program Time:** On-going

**Number of Participants:** Everyone

**Number of Friends/Volunteers needed:** 1 dedicated Coordinator, one back-up

**How/Notes:** Think paparazzi movie premier, or spring blooms, perhaps a lot of glitz and shine. Any décor that stands out, but still compliments and honors the library.

An every other day to every few days social media feed with a short review will create the desired "buzz" to get patrons into the library. And, everyone knows, you can't just take one! The new material pick-up will be followed by a browse and more check-outs!

# #184 – Library bookmark design contest

Creating a sense of ownership and belonging in the library is what a Friends of the Library group should be all about. A means to achieve the goal – let a patron design a bookmark that will be mass produced and the library staff will give away at checkout. There are many free bookmarks that are sent by publishers as promotional materials. Just set those aside for a bit and focus on the fantastic talents within the community.

**Target Audience:** Everyone

**Things needed:**
- A set of guidelines (see below for a sample)
- Age group categories (optional, but encouraged. Or just limit to 12 & under or 13-17 etc.)
- Theme (optional)
- Judges

**Prep Time:** Only to put together the promotional materials and judge

**Program Time:** Give two weeks

**Number of Participants:** Limitless

**Number of Friends/Volunteers needed:** 2-3 for judging

**How/Notes:** Do something like this: Instructions – In the box, create a bookmark that best depicts the library (or Theme: the Library's 100th birthday, our town, our town's Whaling Days etc.).

Guidelines:
- The entire drawing must fit in the box
- No foul language or vulgar depictions are allowed (as judged by the judges)
- Utilize any medium, but remember that the bookmark will be printed.

- All work must be original
- Include spaces for name, age and phone number

Make it all fit in here.

*After proper food, shelter, and love, there is nothing more important to a child than a library. It certainly was the most important place to me in my childhood."*
*Tod Davies*

# Chapter 7 - Keep the money flowing – Fundraising ideas

Programs and library improvements can't happen without at least a little bit of money. Start by visiting the Vision and Mission statements, then decide what funds are anticipated throughout the year. With the funds needed in mind, look to this section for ideas on how to achieve income while still honoring the Vision and Mission statements. Fundraising is a year-round activity and should have its own development plan.

For example: The Mission statement for the year is to increase reading in the community through innovative reading and entertainment programs. For this mission consider looking for grants (Program #190), the Band Jam (Program #188) and Book Sale (Program #195). Or a Mission statement that aims to increase community involvement in the arts might consider the Sidewalk chalk art contest (Program #187) and the Photography photo challenge and art show (Program #192).

The fundraising events don't always have to have a direct tie-in to the Vision and Mission statements, but it does add cohesion and focus on the goals if it can be achieved. Consider how the Friends will be "branded." Develop a unique and recognizable logo to create a visual picture in people's minds.

After any fundraising event, host an After Action Review or (AAR). The AAR is an opportunity to talk about what was expected to happen, what went right (sustain), what went wrong (improve), and suggested changes for the next time a similar event is conducted. Keep good notes, so that a change in personnel doesn't mean starting everything all over again.

Don't forget about other funding avenues such as:
- An on-line giving campaign
- Providing information to patrons about tributes and memorials

- Planned giving in estate planning

Effective fundraising is more about establishing and maintaining relationships than it will ever be about the money generated.

Showing appreciation in a meaningful way to the generous donors will be appreciated long after the money has been used. Saying "Thank You!" matters more than anything else.

*"Civilized nations build libraries; lands that have lost their soul close them down."* — *Toby Forward*

# #185 – Giving tree of services or materials

Many people would love to help an organization but get hung up on the uncertainty of where their cash donation will go. Or, they'd like to offer to help, but are worried about getting roped into a long-term "How do I gracefully get out of this?" commitment. Make it simple and specifically ask for help with a giving tree, board, elephant, banner, or whatever works at your specific location.

**Target Audience:** Everyone

**Things needed:**
- A Coordinator
- Small pictures or descriptions of needed items or services
- Laminating paper (optional)
- Prominent display space

**Prep Time:** This is mostly a one-time set-up, then time to make new placards as needed.

**Program Time:** On-going

**Number of Participants:** N/A

**Number of Friends/Volunteers needed:** 1 Coordinator to make the request postings and keep track of donations resulting from requests.

**How/Notes:** Make placards approximately 3"x3." For materials: print a small picture of the item and note the format needed (audio, large print, paperback, playaway)
Type in the largest print possible to fit on the placards requested services:
- Need front steps scrubbed
- Need reference section books moved down two shelves
- Need help with updating website or website design

Make sure to include a summary of items and services donated for the annual newsletter (Program #177)

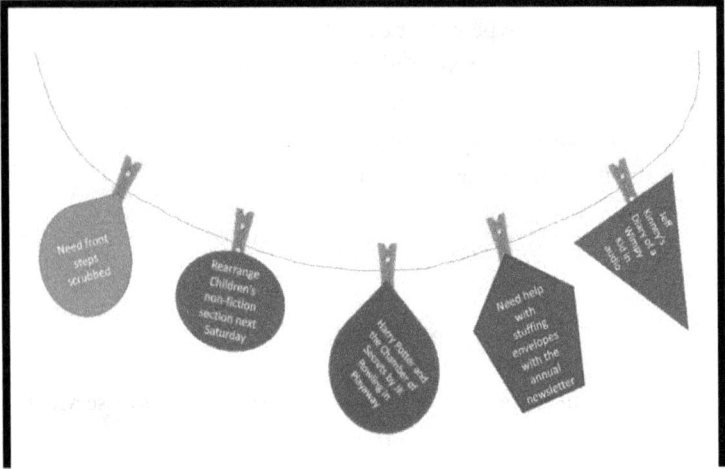

# #186 – Donation box

They are everywhere, which should also include the library circulation desk. Purchase a small acrylic donation box that folks can drop a few coins in and stand back in shock and awe at how quickly the box pays for itself and brings additional revenue into the library coffers.

**Target Audience:** Everyone

**Things needed:**
- Small acrylic box or other container suitable for dropping coins into
- A sign or placard stating what the money will go to "Support the Friends of the Library" or "Electronic Reader Board Fund" etc.

**Prep Time:** Minimal to purchase or make the box and create the sign.

**Program Time:** On-going

**Number of Participants:** Hopefully everyone

**Number of Friends/Volunteers needed:** 1 to empty and keep track of the money generated. Recommend utilizing the same person who handles the funds for the book sale. How about the Treasurer of the Friends?

**How/Notes:** Empty the box at least once a month, preferably right before the Friends meeting so the revenue per month is accurately tracked.

Make sure to buy or make a style that locks and can be fastened to the desk.

# #187 – Sidewalk chalk art contest

A sidewalk chalk art contest can be a fundraiser or just a "fun" raiser. Either way, encouragement of artistic expression will bring people into the library for ideas of all kinds. All it takes is a spark. The fundraiser part can be an entrance fee for the artists, or voting for a People's Choice award. Depending on the size of the space available, consider categories for entrants: 12 & under, Adults, Teams

**Target Audience:** Everyone

**Things needed:**
- A Coordinator/Leader
- An agreement/application. Make sure to note that the art must be suitable for all eyes to see. Be specific on restrictions if needed
- A sidewalk – this event can still be conducted without one, just use butcher paper and markers instead. Consider making this the rain option.
- Chalk (provide or have artists bring their own – or allow both)
- Judges
- Prizes
- Good weather. Go with history. 3-4 "no rain" days are needed.
- Placards for assigned spots (recommend utilizing plastic table tents)
- Voting boxes (optional) recommend selling tickets (votes) for 25 cents or more each for the People's Choice award. This works very well if the top vote getter "splits the pot" with the library. This method will motivate the artists to encourage their friends and family to "come on down and vote for me!"

**Prep Time:** Depending on how big the swath of sidewalk being used, someone will need to clean it. Other than that, prep time is dedicated to advertising, registration and shopping for supplies.

**Program Time:** Limit participants to a few hours to finish their creations. Then, plan on about an hour for judging and prize presentations. Event goers can vote any time.

**Number of Participants:** Varies depending on how much sidewalk is available, making sure to assign only every other section so artists have room to move around.

**Number of Friends/Volunteers needed:** This program could work with as little as one Coordinator/Leader, but if the program is a large event, or part of another event, there should be plenty of volunteers on hand to sell voting tickets and discuss the program with attendees.

**How/Notes:** Look to the high school art department or Parks & Recreation for support and advertising emphasis. Once started, this could be an annual event by itself or part of the library's birthday party, city side-walk sale or other community event.

Add in a side-walk book sale (Program #195) and sell food to generate more revenue.

# #188 – Band Jam

Local bands LOVE opportunities that give them public exposure. Whether they are polished and locally famous, or just starting out, most bands jump at any chance to play. For this fundraiser, the bands play for free, the people listen for free, but buy food and "votes" for their favorite bands. Couple this event on a nice day with the Minute to Win It® fundraiser (Program #193) and everyone will have a blast.

**Target Audience:** Everyone

**Things needed:**
- A Coordinator
- A covered space for the bands to perform
- Electricity (check load requirements vs. load availability)
- Food service, plus all of the necessary serving and permits that go along with the chosen food (or charge vendors to come in)
- Contract – as this program is aimed at everyone, recommend including in the contract what is acceptable and not acceptable for music lyrics and attire. Also a release of liability in case of an incident.
- Voting tickets and buckets with the name of each band
- Cash box
- Portable restrooms (optional)
- Awnings
- Extra trash cans
- Hand washing stations (optional)

**Prep Time:** Time to put together the food and set up the band area. The more helpers available, the faster it will go.

**Program Time:** Depends on the number of bands. It is nice to have an hour set time with a ½ hour transition time. 3 bands = 4 ½ hour event, 4 bands = 6 hour event.

**Number of Participants:** Limited only by the space available

**Number of Friends/Volunteers needed:** Recommend at least 3 times the number of bands participating (food, voting, trash patrol) & designate shifts if needed. Set-up and tear-down crews are needed too.

**How/Notes:** Consider a "split the pot" with the winning vote getter. This method will encourage the bands to reach out to their fan base to bring in patrons.

This event works best at a library or community center with a lawn or large parking area.

Most bands have their own sound equipment, but work with them to see, what, if anything, they'll need prior to the event. Best not to have too many surprises!

Add in a 50/50 raffle and sell tickets throughout the event.

Finally – open the library! And, make sure someone is on-hand in the library to answer questions from new patrons. There will surely be people who come in and say that they've never been in before.

# #189 – Silent auction

A silent auction is a ton of work. But, it is typically a large money maker and if done once a year, it will become a regular event that people look forward to. It is also a nice way for local businesses and artisans to get their work/product to a new audience through donated items or gift certificates for services. This is an "all hands on deck" event that if done well, will be well attended and appreciated in the community.

**Target Audience:** Everyone

**Things needed:**
- A Coordinator
- One person designated to organize and keep track of donations and the value of donations
- A well-crafted letter to the local businesses explaining what is going on and how their donation will be used
- Entertainment – consider dance, music, or vocal students, or other skill demonstrations (Program #134) who will bring their parents and grandparents to see them perform, then stay to enjoy the festivities and bid on items.
- Baskets and wrapping supplies
- A board to display copies of donated gift certificates (the real ones may "walk out")
- Bid sheets (state what is in the basket, bag or box, who donated it, the approximate value, starting bid and required bid increment – For example: Movie night basket – 5 movies, goodies, popcorn. Donated by the Wheeler Family. Value $50.00. Starting bid (go with a third of the value) – 17.00. Bid increment $2.00). Then provide space for a name, telephone number and bid amount. Make sure to number the sheet and the basket, so just in case they get mixed up, they can be put back together.
- Great advertising
- Decorations

- Refreshments (go the easy route and have Friends donate cookies, or purchase a cake), coffee, tea, punch
- Napkins, cups, forks (for cake)
- Music (optional but recommended)
- Door prizes (optional but will keep people at the venue and the longer they stay, the more likely the bids will go up) Give these out periodically throughout the event to keep patrons in attendance longer.

**Prep Time:** A lot of prep time goes into an event like this. The advertising is the first piece, then the sorting and repackaging of donations, creation of the bid sheets and gift certificate board. Coordination of refreshments and entertainment, and contacting bid winners after the event (if they don't stay and pay at the end of the event).

**Program Time:** 4 hours

**Number of Participants:** Limited only by space and fire code

**Number of Friends/Volunteers needed:** Depending on the size of the venue, volunteers will be needed to make announcements, man the refreshment table, monitor bid sheets, monitor trash, take money at the end and during the event if other items are for sale, and take care of last minute details. A minimum of 5 volunteers are needed at the event.

**How/Notes:** Consider selling other items at the event too. Think about logo'd items (Program #191) chocolate or other candy (Program #198) and the book sale (Program #195). Also, be sure to put out the giving tree of needed services and materials (Program #185), as well as the donation box (Program #186).

Make sure to have plenty of trash receptacles around the venue.

Put writing utensils at each bid sheet.
Make sure to publicly thank donors, as well as providing a written individual thank you.

Have the annual newsletter on-hand so donors and bidders can see where their money went this year and will go next year.

Keep the mood festive and light, so that the good feelings translate into generosity for the library.

# #190 – Grants

What if the Friends or Teen Council wanted to start a delivery service (Program #181)? Or someone wants to produce audio versions of duplicate children's books for the library? "Wish it, Dream it, Do it" A great phrase – if the money is available. If it isn't, and the idea is solid and well thought out, consider applying for a grant from one of the many generous organizations, businesses and foundations in this great land of ours.

**Target Audience:** Those interested

**Things needed:**
- A Coordinator/Leader
- A grant resource
- A writing and submission team of volunteers

**Prep Time:** Prep time is dedicated to searching for the right grant and writing the submission according to submission guidelines.

**Program Time:** N/A

**Number of Participants:** N/A

**Number of Friends/Volunteers needed:** Will depend on the grant sought

**How/Notes:** The following is a representative list of a few current options at the time of publication:

*http://www.ala.org/alsc/awardsgrants/profawards/candlewickli ghttheway* - An American Library Association grant that is $3,000 to assist a library in conducting outreach to underserved populations through either a new program or an expansion of a current project.

*http://grants.kidsgardening.org/2014-youth-garden-grant* - Kid Gardening sponsors this grant which consists of a prize of a $500 gift certificate to the Gardening with Kids online store, a tool package from Ames, plant starts from Bonne Plants, two (2) Growums Garden Kits, a raised bed from Rustic Cedar and a seed donation from High Mowing Seeds.

*http://arts.gov/grants-organizations/our-town/grant-program-description* - The National Endowment for the Arts sponsors this grant program subject to available funding. The idea is to create a more cohesive town dedicated to the arts. A program like moss graffiti (Program #44) might fit well into this grant category.

*http://www.legochildrensfund.org/Guidelines.html* - Lego offers grants for projects that focus on early childhood education and development that is directly related to creativity, and for technology and communication projects that advance learning opportunities. Consider this grant for programs like the Lego® building demonstration program (Program #12), or expansion of the How things work series (Program #4) into building too. Also the Film-making workshop (Program #43) would fit into the guidelines of this grant. Oodles of options with this grant.

*http://wishyouwellfoundation.org/apply* - The Wish You Well Foundation offers grants for programs that have the focus of "Supporting family literacy in the United States by fostering and promoting the development and expansion of new and existing literacy and educational programs." Programs like Read to animals (Program #5), the Computer classes (Program #77), Conversational Language Series (Program #104) or Creative Writing Workshop (Program #38) could be expanded under the guidelines of this grant.

# #191 – Logo'd Items

Some Friends groups design their own logo & use it extensively to promote themselves and the library. Design a cool logo and slap it on everything from mugs, latte cups and book bags to eReader covers, hats & shirts.

**Target Audience:** Everyone

**Things needed:**
- A great logo
- A great supplier
- Space to display and store items
- A feel for what to sell

**Prep Time:** A little research goes a long way when making decisions on logo'd items to sell. For example: Is the library located next to a John Deere Dealership which gives away free hats? Then, hats might not be a great choice.

**Program Time:** Ongoing

**Number of Participants:** Hopefully many

**Number of Friends/Volunteers needed:** 1 to manage inventory

**How/Notes:**
Recommend creating a relationship with a supplier who can logo many different items. This way, the graphics set-up fee only needs to be paid once.

Depending on the price, a one color logo will usually give the highest profit margin, especially on larger runs of product.

For an initial order of t-shirts, sweatshirts or jackets, try a pre-order form so that the sizes are correct. If a pre-order gets to the minimum order, there won't be leftovers to store. Those who pre-purchased can wear their items, which will create interest. Continuing with pre-order forms will eliminate an abundance of inventory that will never sell.

# #192 – Photography photo challenge and art show

Think about fun topics for a photography challenge. For example:
- The best thing about (this town)(summer)(school)(this town's festival)
- Nature's alphabet
- Still lifes
- Action shots
- Planking

Whatever the topic, amateur photographers will look forward to showing off their photos, county fair style. Put out the challenge, give a timeframe and be amazed by the creativity of participants. Offer prizes to increase the number of participants and offer refreshments at the art show.

**Target Audience:** Everyone

**Things needed:**
- A Coordinator
- A set of rules - keep them simple.
- Categories for entries. For example (Youth under 12, Teens 12-18, Adults 18+)
- Photo display easels or other method for displaying the photos (matted and wall mounted on free standing cubicle partitions will allow for more photos displayed)
- Placards to show name, category
- Judges - Look to the high school art teacher, a photo studio owner, local professional freelance photographers, or the newspaper photo journalist
- Prizes – Try for donations (photo bag, photo processing gift certificates, photo editing software, cameras, camera equipment, photo albums, other gift certificates)
- Ribbons like the ones used at county fairs (optional)
- Voting bins (see How/Notes)

- Refreshments (optional but recommended)

**Prep Time:** Prep time is three-fold. Initial set-up is in advertising the contest/challenge. Then, sorting and arranging the entrants for judging. Finally, taking time to set up the display of photos for the art show.

**Program Time:** Give entrants 30-60 days (recommend 30 days otherwise they'll forget) to submit their photos. Then, the art show itself (which could include a few demonstrations like cartooning (Program #60), manga/anime (Program #53), jewelry making (Program #54)). A run time should be about 2 to 3 hours.

**Number of Participants:** Limited only by space and fire code

**Number of Friends/Volunteers needed:** Several throughout both the photography challenge and the art show

**How/Notes:**
- Add a "People's Choice" award by placing voting bins in front of the photos. People vote with money (coffee cans work great for this). Or, if a vertical display is used, consider using a ticket system where attendees purchase votes in the form of tickets and put the tickets into zip-style bags with a re-enforced hole cut into them. Hang the bags next to the photos and mark each so that everyone knows where to put their vote.
- It may not be possible to display all of the entrants in the art show due to space, so participants should be aware of the possibility.
- Award the prizes and People's Choice award close to the end of the show to keep "votes" coming in.
- Fourth of July parade go right by your location? Annual Side-walk sale just down the street? Tie-in to another community event.
- And make sure to have plenty of seating available. People enjoy art at their own pace.

- Consider offering other activities too, such as: paint book ends (Program #119), make book plates (Program #128) or Zentangle (Program #46).

*"Libraries are the latest fashion for the brain "E. Jean Carroll*

# #193 – Minute-to-Win-It® games

Family fun and a couple of bucks for the library – a winning combination. This is not a mega dollar fundraiser, but patrons will have so much fun, it could easily become an annual or semi-annual event.

**Target Audience:** Everyone

**Things needed:**
- Tables
- Tickets
- Ticket buckets
- Prizes (tattoos, stickers, small wrapped candies, pencils)
- Small bags to carry the prizes (look for a local donor)
- Plenty of space
- Signs and instructions for each game
- The household items needed for each game
- Refreshments (optional, but allowing vendors could be a nice addition to the fundraiser)

**Prep Time:** It will take a few hours to set everything up. Signs and instructions will need to be made ahead of time too.

**Program Time:** 2-4 hours

**Number of Participants:** Hopefully many

**Number of Friends/Volunteers needed:** Several – at least one per game and additional to rotate for breaks.
**How/Notes:** This event is best as a "buy and exchange" system. Sell tickets for 25 - 50 cents each, or discounted in bulk, or perhaps a "play all you want" wristband for a certain price, and make each game 1 ticket (2 tickets for the 2 person games). Volunteers at the stations need only collect the tickets, making the process faster and easier to manage. Small prizes should be available for people who win.

Recommend volunteers preview the game they are facilitating at *http://www.nbc.com* prior to starting their assignment, so they fully understand the requirements and can explain the game to participants.

Consider allowing the younger set, say age under age 10, to have to do half the requirement. Example Nutstacker would be 5 nuts instead of 10.

Make posters to explain the rules, so the game facilitator/volunteer doesn't have to explain each time.

Games suggested:
- **Breakfast Scramble** (use a long table so more than one player can be supported at a time)
  - o Need: cereal boxes cut and laminated. Recommend two 16 piece, and two 8 piece puzzles (for the younger participants)
  - o How: At the start signal, participants turn over their pieces and re-assemble the cereal box picture.
- **Flip your lid** – flip a cup from the edge of the table onto a bottle
  - o Need: plastic cups and a glass bottle
  - o How: At the start signal, participants attempt to flip a cup from the edge of the table onto the ·bottle.
- **Extreme Nutstacker**
  - o Need: 10 metal 5/8" nuts, wooden cutting board, 1 chopstick, tape for a foul line on chopstick
  - o How: At the start signal, participants slide nuts onto chopstick so they're all touching. Player stacks all nuts on the cutting board in a stack of 10 that remains standing for 3 seconds. ** Players hands cannot touch beyond the foul line.
- **Double Trouble**
  - o Need: Container of ping pong balls, 2 wide-rimmed pint glasses, table

- How: Set glasses 2 ½ feet apart. At the start signal, participant throws both balls at once, bouncing them on the table and landing them in the glasses. Both have to land in a single throw. If there is a coveted prize, make it available at this station.

- **Caddy Stack**
  - Need: 3 golf balls, level surface
  - How: At the start signal, participants attempt to stack 3 golf balls free standing. ** Must remain standing for 3 seconds.

- **Chop Stack**
  - Need: chopsticks, 4 lip balm tubes, table
  - How: Lay the lip balm tubes on the table. At the start signal, participants attempt to stack the tubes on the table vertically one on top of another. ** Must remain standing for 3 seconds.

- **Loner**
  - Need: 20 or more marbles, 1 unsharpened pencil, foul line, clean, level floor and a back-board or catch area
  - How: Stand unsharpened pencil on end 15' from foul line. Participant lies on stomach behind the foul line. At the start signal, participants roll marbles, one at a time toward the pencil in an attempt to knock over the pencil. ** Release of marble must be behind the foul line (like in bowling).

- **Movin' on up**
  - Need: 39 blue cups, 1 red cup (or any other colors with the same ratio)
  - How: Stack cups so the stack of 39 is on top of the lone red one. At the start signal, participants transfer one cup at a time from the top of the stack to the bottom alternating hands, and wins when the red cup is on top.

- Office Tennis (this is a Team Game)
    - Need: 2 clipboards, balled up pieces of paper, wastepaper basket.
    - How: Participants stand facing each other. At the start signal, participants begin batting the balled up piece of paper back and forth toward the wastepaper basket in an attempt to land the ball in the basket. ** Drops go back to the beginning. The game is won when a piece of paper is in the wastepaper basket.
- Penny hose
    - Need: A pair of pantyhose (a few extra pairs too because as time goes on, they'll either tear or get too stretched out), 2 pennies
    - How: Place a penny in each leg so that they end up in the toe. At the start signal, participants work one hand into each leg of the hose. The hands cannot touch each other. The game is complete and won when both pennies are out of the pantyhose.
- Rapid fire
    - Need: six empty, clean and dry soda pop cans, a bunch of elastic rubber bands (doesn't matter if they are all the same size or not, a bowl or container to hold the bands so that participants can easily reach them, a table and a marked starting line. Place the cans upright in a pyramid shape on the table 8 feet from the starting line.
    - How: At the start signal, participants grab rubber bands and shoot them one at a time (stretch and slingshot style) at the soda pop can pyramid in an attempt to knock over the cans. The game is won when all of the cans are knocked over.
- Speed eraser
    - Need: lots of unsharpened pencils, seven drinking cups that are heavy enough that they won't fall over when hit by a flying pencil, a long table, a bowl or cup to hold the pencils. Line up the cups

so that they do not touch (at least 8" in between is preferred).

- o How: At the start signal, participants grab pencils and bounce them on the eraser end, one at a time, so that they land in the cup. Any pencil that bounces out of the cup does not count. The game is complete when each cup holds a pencil.

- **Temper tantrum**
  - o Need: Two pedometers attached to a ribbon or elastic that can easily be transferred from person to person, but will stay on the feet. Recommend having a few extra pedometers on hand in case one breaks.
  - o How: At the start signal, participants lay on their backs and kick their legs up and down trying to accumulate the designated number of steps. The game is won when the number on the pedometer exceeds the designated number.

- **Wet Ball**
  - o Need: Balloons (regular standard size birthday balloons are sufficient), a bucket or container to hold the balloons, a regular outdoor garbage can, and a spray bottle with some gusto (enough to propel the balloon but not break it), foul line. Place the garbage can about 10-12 feet from the foul line, the bucket of balloons near the foul line, and fill the spray bottle with water. ** If this game is played indoors, consider laying a tarp on the floor and having a towel on hand to periodically dry off the tarp.
  - o How: At the start signal, participants grab a balloon and the spray bottle. They throw the balloon into the air and spray water at the balloon in an attempt to maneuver it to the trash can. The game is won when the balloon is in the trash can. If the balloon breaks, the participant goes back to the beginning and gets another one.

# #194 – Food for thought

Food for Thought is the name of one of my all-time favorite places to be. A bistro across the street from the University of Montana campus in Missoula, MT. I've always thought it would make a great fundraising title – so catchy. For this program, the library couples with a local restaurant and volunteers their time and efforts for a portion of the night's proceeds.

**Target Audience:** Everyone

**Things needed:**
- A Coordinator
- A willing restaurant
- An agreement
- A marketing campaign (use social media and local media outlets to get the word out)
- Coupons (optional)
- Volunteers

**Prep Time:** Prep time is dedicated to coordination and marketing

**Program Time:** 1 to 3 nights

**Number of Participants:** Hopefully many

**Number of Friends/Volunteers needed:** Will depend on the arrangement with the restaurant

**How/Notes:** It is likely that anyone who participates as a volunteer will have to have a Food Handler's permit. However, there are jobs where that certification may not be required. Make sure to discuss needed certifications with the restaurant manager to avoid surprises.

There are some restaurants who will partner with groups without the groups actually having to come in and make a mess of things. The Friends will need to saturate the community with coupons and advertising though and the restaurant will provide proceeds from the diners who either bring in the coupon or say that they heard about the event.

Many restaurants have the needed agreement forms together already, hopefully there is one nearby.

# #195 – Book sale

If there is available dedicated space, a standing used book sale is a great idea. A neatly arranged and organized sale will bring in a steady income for the Friends. Consider an annual side-walk sale too, and it's time to sing... "We're in the money!"

**Target Audience:** Everyone

**Things needed:**
- Space
- Books, and other media
- Good signage
- Additional storage space for extra books and materials

**Prep Time:** Spend time putting together a quality display, then depending on the size of the display, a Friend will need to spend a few minutes to a half an hour a week straightening and arranging.

**Program Time:** On-going

**Number of Participants:** Hopefully everyone

**Number of Friends/Volunteers needed:** 1-2 – Volunteers can rotate and each take a two-week "shift."

**How/Notes:** Recommend standing prices. All hardback, paperback, children's, audio etc. are a certain price unless otherwise marked. Produce signage and clearly mark materials that are specially priced.

Don't try to cram too much into the space. Leave room around the materials so browsers can see them better.

It is extremely important to maintain the book sale so that it stays neat and orderly. If it is unkempt it will be unvisited – guaranteed.

# #196 – Plant sale

This is another community building event, more so than a mega-fundraiser. A plant sale highlights the local growers and the library's resources. Add on a free seed starter to get the youngest participants interested.

**Target Audience:** Everyone

**Things needed:**
- A partnership – look for patron volunteers, the high school biology or botany club, or the local garden club for donations and volunteers
- Advertising
- Plenty of space
- Signs with prices and information
- Money till and change
- Tables and chairs

**Prep Time:** About 1 ½ hours to set up tables, lay out plants and make signs

**Program Time:** A few hours – recommend a 3 hour timeframe on a Saturday morning

**Number of Participants:** Hopefully many

**Number of Friends/Volunteers needed:** At least 2-3

**How/Notes:** Recommend several categories: Herbs, Vegetables, Perennials, Annuals, Succulents etc.

How about taking orders for holiday wreaths or poinsettias during the sale? Or have on-hand Memorial Day wreaths for sale too. Recommend this sale be conducted in conjunction with a larger event like a large scale book sale (Program #195) or seed and bulb exchange (Program #175) to increase interest.

# #197 - "Sock Hop"

A fantastic "fun" raiser. The premise: Host a '50's style dance and have fun dancing. This could be a fundraiser for the library if the event was large enough. Have an entrance fee, but offer a few dollars off the ticket price for a sock donation which will go to a local shelter or school.

**Target Audience:** Everyone

**Things needed:**
- A planning committee
- Music
- Decorations
- Refreshments
- Games (optional)
- Raffle items
- Photo area, school dance style (this could be part of the fundraiser, or just for fun)

**Prep Time:** Will depend on how extravagant the party. Decorations take time to put up, and advertising will be important for this event.

**Program Time:** 4 hours

**Number of Participants:** Limited only by space and fire code. Recommend pre-selling tickets so numbers can be gauged for refreshments.

**Number of Friends/Volunteers needed:** Several prior to and during the event

**How/Notes:** This is a party, so it will be as elaborate or as subdued as you choose.

Consider the following:
- How about a 50/50 raffle?

- What about contests with prizes to get everyone in the spirit? Best "Greaser," "Nerd," "Soda Jerk," cutest couple, "car hop," "poodle skirt girl"
- Maybe a photo booth that looks like a car at a drive-in movie, or diner booth?

The more outrageous, the more memorable. The more memorable, the more sponsors and money to be made!

Seek corporate sponsorship and offer discounted tickets to their employees.

Partner with a local restaurant if alcohol is part of the plan.

Add in a classic car show to draw car enthusiasts and cars of the era.

# #198 – Chocolate or other candy sale

Purchased or made, few people can resist a sweet treat now and then. And, when the urge hits and there happens to be a lovely display 'right there,' the answer often is "YES! I'd like a candy please." This fundraiser takes little effort and pays pretty well.

**Target Audience:** Everyone

**Things needed:**
- A dedicated volunteer or supplier
- Candy making supplies (if homemade)
- Packaging supplies (if homemade)
- Display and sign

**Prep Time:** Time to make or purchase the candy and create the display

**Program Time:** On-going

**Number of Participants:** Hopefully many & often

**Number of Friends/Volunteers needed:** 1 to make/manage

**How/Notes:** A word of caution about homemade candies – please check with the county health department for any requirements and work hard ensure the utmost in quality and cleanliness standards are maintained.

# #199 – "Soup"er Bowl Party

Not everyone is a football fan. Embrace the non-fans with this fun fundraiser when all the other fans are whoopin' it up in front of the TV. Or, use this fundraiser to kick-off a festive start to football season.

**Target Audience:** Anyone interested

**Things needed:**
- A variety of soups, breads and crackers
- Bowls and spoons
- Salt & pepper
- Napkins
- Adequate power to support several soup pots
- Music (optional)

**Prep Time:** About an hour to get soup pots set up and arrange space + soup making time.

**Program Time:** Run for a few hours and patrons can come whenever they want. The Super Bowl is typically about a 4 hour event, so plan around that timeframe, if appropriate.

**Number of Participants:** Hopefully many

**Number of Friends/Volunteers needed:** At least 2-3 with one solely dedicated to handling money

**How/Notes:** Pick a different day if the turn-out looks as if it would be too low. There are a few ways to run this event.

Consider:
- Charge for a soup meal with provided bowls
- Partner with the high school art department and have them provide bowls made by students. Patrons then buy the bowls for a much higher fee with a bottomless bowl option.

- Or as another twist – marry these two options. Provide disposable bowls for the soup, but have a silent auction for the bowls made by the students. Either way, split the proceeds with the art department.

Make sure to consult the county health department for food service requirements.

*"The America I love still exists at the front desks of our public libraries." - Kurt Vonnegut*

# #200 – Torture the librarian

This fundraiser works only if the library is fortunate enough to have a fun-loving, willing librarian or library staff member or local leader available – perhaps the high school principal? Come up with a few horrifically fun "tortures" for patrons to vote on, then, make sure there are plenty of pictures to share!

**Target Audience:** Everyone

**Things needed:**
- Willing participants
- A list of deliciously horrible things to do and whatever supplies are needed to support the deliciously horrible thing (See How/Notes)
- Money collection containers and a safe place to put them
- Camera

**Prep Time:** Prep time is dedicated to making the donation containers, counting the money, and preparing the deliciously horrible "torture."

**Program Time:** Run this fundraiser for a week or two before the event where the "torture" will occur.

**Number of Participants:** Hopefully everyone

**Number of Friends/Volunteers needed:** 1-2

**How/Notes:** Have the "torture" coincide with another library event so that as many people as possible can enjoy seeing their favorite librarian or local leader "tortured." What is great about having this fundraiser coincide with another event is, it provides entertaining free publicity for the other event. This program would pair nicely with the Library Birthday party (Program #180), Sidewalk Chalk Art Contest (Program #187), end of Summer Reading party (not a program in this book, because nearly every library already does this), Band Jam (Program #188).

Get the "volunteer" involved in what they may be willing to do. Here are a few deliciously horrible ideas:

- Kiss a pig, frog or something else icky that won't bite
- Dye hair an outrageous color
- Walk on stilts
- Sing a silly song or do a funny dance every time a bell rings during the event
- Wear clothes backwards
- Walk around in a snorkel and swim fins all day

Consider this for the Teen Council – they could garner a ton of enthusiasm for an event like this one and would have more wild ideas than mine.

# #201 – Grocery bagging

The grocery bagger is a long-standing customer service tradition. Some grocers (especially local, non-chain grocers) are open to the idea of allowing baggers to come in and work for tips for their particular cause. Work with a local grocer, distribute flyers in the store and the library and through social media explaining who you are and where the money will go, and have some fun!

**Target Audience:** Everyone shopping

**Things needed:**
- A Coordinator
- Volunteers – to bag and to hand out flyers
- Some bagging skills (the grocer may give a short lesson on proper bagging technique – no eggs on the bottom!)
- Tip buckets (coffee cans work well)

**Prep Time:** Prep time is dedicated to coordination and flyer development and distribution

**Program Time:** A few shifts throughout one day or a weekend

**Number of Participants:** Hopefully many

**Number of Friends/Volunteers needed:** At least 3-4 baggers and flyer distributers + Coordinator

**How/Notes:** This is a fantastic Teen Council project. They can do the coordination and the work and use the money to fund programs of interest to them (see Chapter 3 for a few ideas).

Discuss with the grocer which day is the busiest, or second busiest and plan on that day.
Make sure baggers are courteous and express thanks to anyone who donates. They should also ask if grocery shoppers would like help out to their cars with their groceries, if appropriate, as safety may be a concern.

# Final Thoughts

So there it is – a compiled list of some ideas to use, or use as a starting point for other ideas, to breathe new life into your library. Remember! These ideas can be adapted for use in Community centers, schools, after-school clubs, senior centers, churches – really, anywhere people get together. Libraries aren't for Shh shing, they are a gathering place for people to gain knowledge and come together as a community.

And remember - if a program is not successful the first time it is presented, look for the reason. Was it at a bad time? Did it conflict with something else in town that appealed to the target audience? Was it advertised poorly? Or, did it just not appeal to anyone. Take all factors into consideration before scrapping the idea. There could be numerous reasons why it didn't work. Solicit feedback and take notes for next time.

I took the time to write this book, because it is important. And, you took the time to read it because it is important to you too. So, go! Go do great works in your community!

Oh, and one last thing...Always under promise and over deliver. So, with that in mind, here's one more:

# #202 – Story time

In this book we've gone way beyond story time, but story time is a classic. It is an entertaining, simple way to get children and care-givers into the library. If it isn't already part of the standard library program list, add it today!

**Target Audience:** 0-5 year olds

**Things needed:**
- A dynamic Storyteller
- Props (if needed)
- Awesome books from the library's collection
- Additional books similar to the story presented available for check-out
- A follow-on activity (if desired)

**Prep Time:** Minimal to arrange space and activity

**Program Time:** 45 minutes to an hour

**Number of Participants:** Limited only by space and fire code

**Number of Friends/Volunteers needed:** 1-2

**How/Notes:** Choose great books and read with enthusiasm!

Invite guest readers in too.

Use props like puppets and felt boards.

Engage participants and ask for their help.

*"Whatever the cost of our libraries, the price is cheap compared to that of an ignorant nation."*

*- Walter Cronkite*